Post-Public Employment

GOOD PRACTICES FOR PREVENTING CONFLICT OF INTEREST

OECD

ORGANISATION FOR ECONOMIC CO-OPERATION AND DEVELOPMENT

The OECD is a unique forum where governments work together to address the economic, social and environmental challenges of globalisation. The OECD is also at the forefront of efforts to understand and to help governments respond to new developments and concerns, such as corporate governance, the information economy and the challenges of an ageing population. The Organisation provides a setting where governments can compare policy experiences, seek answers to common problems, identify good practice and work to co-ordinate domestic and international policies.

The OECD member countries are: Australia, Austria, Belgium, Canada, Chile, the Czech Republic, Denmark, Finland, France, Germany, Greece, Hungary, Iceland, Ireland, Italy, Japan, Korea, Luxembourg, Mexico, the Netherlands, New Zealand, Norway, Poland, Portugal, the Slovak Republic, Slovenia, Spain, Sweden, Switzerland, Turkey, the United Kingdom and the United States. The European Commission takes part in the work of the OECD.

OECD Publishing disseminates widely the results of the Organisation's statistics gathering and research on economic, social and environmental issues, as well as the conventions, guidelines and standards agreed by its members.

ISBN 978-92-64-05669-5 (print)
ISBN 978-92-64-05670-1 (PDF)

Also available in French: *L'emploi d'après mandat : Bonnes pratiques en matière de prévention des conflits d'intérêts*

Corrigenda to OECD publications may be found on line at: *www.oecd.org/publishing/corrigenda*.

Foreword

The horizontal movement of personnel between the public and private sectors, known as the "revolving door" phenomenon, has supported labour market dynamism and the development of skills and competencies. However, it has also raised the risk of post-public employment conflict-of-interest situations. These may result in the misuse of commercially sensitive information or privileged access, for example, when ex-officials lobby their former government institutions. Moving from career-based to position-based public service particularly intensifies these risks.

Post-public employment was identified by the Public Governance Committee as an emerging concern during the review of progress made in implementing the 2003 OECD Council Recommendation on Guidelines for Managing Conflict of Interest in the Public Service. Subsequently, the Committee reviewed governance arrangements to prevent and manage potential conflict-of-interest situations involving officials who have left public office.

This report provides, in line with identified good practice, guidance to policy makers and managers on how to review and modernise rules, policies and practices for preventing and managing conflict of interest in post-public employment. Chapters 1 and 2 examine the context and problem areas such as: seeking future private sector employment while still in public office, switching sides to represent opposite interests in an ongoing procedure, re-engaging former officials as consultants, using insider information for personal benefit or lobbying government institutions where the official formerly worked. Chapters 3 and 4 present principles, a framework and good practices for managing post-public employment conflict of interest. Chapter 5 offers a detailed case study based on Norway's experience and lessons learned in developing and implementing distinct post-public employment guidelines for politicians and the public service.

This report is a contribution of the Public Governance Committee to the efforts of the OECD for cleaner, fairer and stronger economies through mapping governance and corruption risks and developing standards for integrity in the public sector. Complementary work of the Committee examines risk areas, in particular the "revolving door" phenomenon in the financial sector, lobbying and public procurement.

The OECD Expert Group on Conflict of Interest conducted a survey of the 30 OECD member countries to identify risk areas and to develop principles and a framework for managing post-public employment conflict of interest. The survey findings and conclusions were discussed in a Special Session of the Expert Group on

Conflict of Interest, then in the workshop on conflict of interest organised within the Global Forum on Public Governance "Building a Cleaner World: Tools and Good Practices to Build a Culture of Integrity" in May 2009 in Paris, France. Representatives of business, trade unions, civil society organisations, academics, international organisations together with governments of non-OECD countries supported the principles and framework.

The report was prepared by János Bertók, Head of the Integrity Unit in the Reform of the Public Sector Division of the Public Governance and Territorial Development Directorate. Christian Vergez, Head of Division, provided guidance to the project. Special thanks are given to the Chair of the OECD Expert Group on Conflict of Interest, Catherine Macquarrie, Associate Commissioner, and to Mary Dawson, Commissioner, Office of the Conflict of Interest and Ethics Commissioner, Canada, for co-chairing the Special Session on Post-Public Employment and for the substantive advice. Assistance in the preparation of the publication was provided by Karena Garnier.

Table of Contents

Annexes to Chapter 5 are available on line at the links below:

5.A1. Post-Employment Guidelines for Politicians:
http://dx.doi.org/10.1787/735516772805

5.A2. Post-Employment Guidelines for the Public Service:
http://dx.doi.org/10.1787/735536866404

5.A3. Ethical Guidelines for the Public Service:
http://dx.doi.org/10.1787/735573105756

Boxes

Figures

Acronyms

ACoBA	Advisory Committee on Business Appointments, United Kingdom
APS	Australian Public Service
APSC	Australian Public Service Commission
CSO	Civil society organisation
DPOH	Designated public office holder
EC	European Commission
EU	European Union
EUR	Euro currency
FAA	Federal Accountability Act, Canada
FAQ	Frequently asked questions
HLOGA	Honest Leadership and Open Government Act, United States
HRM	Human resource management
ICT	Information and communication technology
IMF	International Monetary Fund
JPY	Japanese yen currency
NGO	Non-governmental organisation
OECD	Organisation for Economic Co-operation and Development
OGE	Office of Government Ethics, United States
PASC	Public Administration Select Committee, House of Commons, United Kingdom
PPP	Public private partnership
SSC	State Services Commission, New Zealand
UK	United Kingdom
US	United States
USD	United States dollars currency
WB	World Bank
WBG	World Bank Group

Executive Summary

There is increased concern about movement of personnel between the public and the private sectors, in particular in times of economic crisis and downsizing. Increased mobility between the two sectors has supported labour-market dynamism in OECD countries. When officials leave public office – either permanently or temporarily – to work in the private or non-profit sectors, however, concerns of impropriety (such as the misuse of "insider information" and position) can put trust in the public service at risk. Causes of increased public and governmental concern about post-public employment conflict of interest include the facts that:

- the public sector has developed close interactions with other sectors which can result in increased risks to integrity, *e.g.* public officials may have unduly cosy relationships with business and non-profit organisations;
- public officials are moving much more frequently, either permanently or temporarily, between public- and private-sector jobs.

Consequently, many countries are making it a priority to review and modernise arrangements to effectively prevent and manage conflict of interest in post-public employment. Most post-public employment offences occur when public officials use information or contacts acquired while in government to benefit themselves, or others, after they leave government. However, despite the use of the term "post-public employment", these offences can also occur before officials actually leave government.*

Major post-public employment problem areas involve public officials when they:

- seek future employment outside the public service;
- conduct post-public employment lobbying back to government institutions;
- switch sides in the same process;
- use "insider information";
- are re-employed in the public service, for example, to do the same tasks they performed in the private or non-profit sectors.

* *Public Integrity and Post-Public Employment: Issues, Remedies and Benchmarks*, GOV/PGC/ETH(2007)3, this scoping paper was prepared by Professor Kenneth Kernaghan, Brock University, Ontario, Canada for discussion at the OECD Expert Group on Conflict of Interest in June 2007 in Paris.

The challenge for governments is to strike an appropriate balance between fostering public integrity through adequate post-public employment instruments and to preserve a reasonable measure of employment freedom to attract experienced and skilful candidates for public office. Experience shows how influential the context is in designing, implementing and enforcing adequate post-public employment measures tailored to properly address the particular problems countries face.

Survey findings show that the vast majority of OECD countries have established basic post-employment standards to avoid conflict-of-interest situations in the public sector. Several countries have even strengthened restrictions in the past years. However, only a few countries have tailored standards to risk areas when, for example, regulators or procurement officials move to the private sector. Enforcing established standards and imposing suitable sanctions remain a challenge for many countries. Ensuring compliance with post-public employment measures can indeed be particularly difficult because most post-public employment offences are committed by public officials who, by leaving the public sector, move somewhat beyond administrative government control.

The Principles for Managing Post-Public Employment Conflict of Interest provide a point of reference for policy makers and managers to review and modernise post-public employment policy and practice. The Principles were designed to support efforts to prevent actual or potential conflict of interest in public office, *e.g.* by requiring that "public officials should not enhance their future private sector employment prospects by giving preferential treatment to potential employers" in decision making. In reviewing their actual arrangements, policy makers may consider systematically examining the extent to which existing regulations, policies and practices can meet the requirements of the principles, as a first step.

Moreover, policy makers may consider the Post-Public Employment Good Practice Framework when developing options for implementation and enforcement instruments and measures. The Framework addresses strategic aspects of managing a post-public employment system and it also provides a structure for developing coherent and comprehensive post-public employment policy and practice. Selected elements of good practices are also presented in the Framework to give concrete examples of options that could be considered as benchmarks.

Key pillars of the Post-Public Employment Good Practice Framework include, in particular:

- The post-public employment system contains the instrument(s) needed to deal effectively with its current and anticipated post-public employment problems and emerging concerns.

- The post-public employment instrument(s) is linked, where feasible, with instrument(s) dealing with conflict of interest in the public sector and with the overall values and integrity framework.
- The post-public employment system covers all entities for which post-public employment is a real or potential problem and meets the distinctive needs of each entity.
- The post-public employment system covers all of the important risk areas for post-public employment conflict of interest.
- The restrictions, in particular the length of time limits imposed on the activities of former public officials, are proportionate to the gravity of the post-public employment conflict-of-interest threat that the officials pose.
- The restrictions and prohibitions contained in the post-public employment system are effectively communicated to all affected parties.
- The authorities, procedures and criteria for making approval decisions in individual post-public employment cases, as well as for appeals against these decisions, are transparent and effective.
- The enforcement sanctions for post-public employment offences are clear and proportional, and are timely, consistently and equitably applied.
- The effectiveness of the policies and practices contained in each post-public employment system is assessed regularly and, where appropriate, is updated and adjusted to emerging concerns.

Dealing with post-public employment problems has been a relatively recent challenge in many OECD countries. However, even countries with established post-public employment frameworks have faced newly emerging concerns – driven by constantly evaluating socio-political contexts – that have forced governments to adjust existing regulations, policies and practices. This book draws attention to reviewed elements of good practices – identified across OECD countries mainly at the national level, but also at the sub-national level – to help future efforts by outlining alternative options as valuable benchmarks and sharing experiences and lessons learned.

A further challenge is to provide evidence on the extent to which formal instruments are implemented and daily practices are effective. As this requires a good understanding of the context, a country study provides further insights on emerging concerns related to post-public employment in the political-administrative context of Norway. Chapter 5 explains the approach taken by the government and steps for developing post-public employment guidelines for both politicians and public servants.

Ambiguity in transition from political to senior civil service positions and from civil service to the private and non-profit sectors has pushed post-public employment issues forward to the Norwegian Parliament. The *Storting* requested reports on existing arrangements and considered it significant to introduce possible restrictions in post-public employment in order to maintain integrity in government. Consequently, the Post-Employment Guidelines for the Public Service were issued for public servants in July 2005, followed by the Ethical Guidelines for the Public Service in September 2005 to modernise the wider framework for promoting integrity in the public service.

In addition to the public servants, a separate set of guidelines, the Post-Employment Guidelines for Politicians was developed for ministers, political secretaries and political advisers. These guidelines came into force almost immediately to cover post-public employment cases of former senior officials after the government transition in November 2005. This case study summarises the main features of the three guidelines and explains how they fit into the Norwegian socio-political and administrative context. It also presents implementing mechanisms and highlights lessons learned in their application in the early years.

Although the provisions on prohibitions and restrictions in the Post-Employment Guidelines are almost identical for politicians and public servants, the approval decision-making process on post-employment cases differs substantially. While approval decisions for public servants remain in the administrative hierarchy, an independent body – the Standing Committee on Outside Political Appointments – was established with the authority to decide in the post-employment cases of ministers, political secretaries and political advisers. As key documents of this procedure are available on the web, information on post-employment cases of former politicians is highly visible: this enables public scrutiny and supports compliance.

This report is integral part of the Public Governance Committee's contribution to the OECD's efforts to promote integrity in the public sector, which involves strategies for mapping governance and corruption risks – *e.g.* procurement, lobbying, conflict of interest and the "revolving door" phenomenon – and develops standards for cleaner, fairer and stronger economies. The Committee is examining the "revolving door" phenomenon in the financial sector.

Chapter 1

Post-public employment: Practices and concerns

This chapter provides the context for post-public employment and explains the nature and implications of major types of post-employment problems. It also defines important terms used throughout this book and sets out the scope and structure of developing principles and good practice framework.

Post-public employment: A practice on the rise

A growing challenge across OECD countries has been how to attract the "best and brightest" workforce to serve the public interest in public organisations. In line with new public management practices, several countries have encouraged movement of personnel between the public sector and the private sector and opened up recruitment in middle and higher-level positions. As a result, movement between sectors is on the rise. For example, over 75% of new entrants in senior positions came from outside the civil service in the United Kingdom and, after a period of four to five years, sought to return to the private or non-profit sectors.

Facilitating the development of civil servants' skills and competencies through gaining experience in the private sector is supported by public opinion in many countries. For example, a French survey indicated 70% support for putting in place a system that obliges civil servants to get experience in the private sector during their career (Institut CSA, 2006). In fact, skill development and "removing barriers to labour market participation has become the key priority for most OECD countries" (OECD, 2006a).

In the past 20 years, most countries have opened up the recruitment of their public services, either through the move towards more position-based systems, with all positions open to outside applicants; the move of parts of their systems to more position-based employment systems (such as in agencies in some systems); or the opening of senior positions to more lateral entries. Even in countries that traditionally have relatively closed career-based systems, *e.g.* Belgium, France, Ireland and Korea, the recruitment of large parts of senior-level positions has been opened up to applicants from the private sector.

Leaving public office, however, also raises legitimate questions about the potential use or misuse of the special knowledge and insights of public officials when they leave office and – either temporarily or permanently – work in the private or not-for-profit sectors. The knowledge of commercially sensitive information, for example, could provide unfair advantage over competitors. Suspicion of impropriety, such as the potential misuse of "insider information" (defined as information not available to the public, such as classified government information, *e.g.* on policy intention, national security, etc.; data on personal privacy; and commercially sensitive information, *e.g.* trade secrets) for the illicit benefit of former public officials is a widely shared concern across OECD countries, as it could endanger confidence in public decisions and public service in general. Post-public employment could become a particularly highly sensitive issue during government transitions or periods of outsourcing and downsizing.

Maintaining citizens' trust in government – a key concern across OECD countries[1] – requires ensuring that officials persistently serve the public interest. What instruments and mechanisms can achieve this aim when public officials leave office? Identifying, preventing and managing conflict of interest (defined as "a conflict between the public duty and private interests of public officials, in which public officials have private-capacity interests which could improperly influence the performance of their official duties and responsibilities" [OECD, 2004, p. 15]) in post-public employment is critical to defending the public interest and controlling potential breaches to integrity when officials leave the public sector, be it temporarily or permanently.

Post-public employment offences occur when public officials use, or appear to use, information or contacts acquired while in government to benefit themselves, or others, after they leave government. However, conflict of interest related to post-employment can also occur before officials actually leave public office. For example, a serving public official can give preferential treatment to a business firm with a view to obtaining employment with that firm after leaving government. If the official is successful in obtaining that employment and leaves government, he or she had an actual conflict-of-interest situation related to post-public employment. The former official, for example, can also use confidential information obtained while in government to the benefit of his or her new employer. Thus, conflict of interest related to post-public employment can arise both from:

- the use of someone's current public office for private gain (*e.g.* making a biased decision to benefit a prospective employer);
- the wrongful exploitation of someone's previous public office (*e.g.* misusing sensitive official information for the illicit benefit of the former public official or his or her new employer).

More examples of what can happen as personnel move between the public and the private sector (otherwise known as the "revolving door" phenomenon) can be found in Box 1.1. The focus of this book, however, will primarily be on the behaviour of former public officials in their relations with public organisations.

Box 1.1. **Movement between the public and private sectors: The "revolving door" phenomenon**

The movement of key actors between the private and public sectors is often called the "revolving door" phenomenon. Executives of corporations and representatives of special interest groups have built up close relationships with government institutions, in particular those that oversee or regulate the sector concerned. Forms of the revolving door phenomenon include:

- *From private sector-to-government revolving door:* the appointment of corporate executives and business lobbyists to key posts in government agencies. This phenomenon, also known as the "reverse revolving door" may establish a pro-business bias in policy formulation and regulatory enforcement in governmental posts that oversee their former industry or employer.
- *From government-to-private sector revolving door:* when public officials move to lucrative private-sector positions in which they may use their government experience and connections – while they are still in office or after leaving public office – to unfairly benefit their new employer (*e.g.* in matters of public procurement, regulatory policy, etc.).
- *From government-to-lobbyist revolving door:* movement of decision makers (*e.g.* former lawmakers and executive-branch officials) to become well-paid advocates and to use the inside connections of former officials to advance the interests of corporate clients.

Source: Revolving Door Working Group (2005), "A Matter of Trust: How the Revolving Door Undermines Public Confidence in Government – and What to Do About It", *www.revolvingdoor.info*.

Concerns: Undermining the public interest

There are several causes of increased public and governmental concern about post-public employment conflict of interest.

First, concern about post-public employment is part of a broader concern in countries around the world about integrity of public officials and, in particular, about bias resulting from conflict of interest in public decision making. The OECD recognised this concern and developed principles and policy recommendations in the form of a Recommendation on Guidelines for Managing Conflict of Interest in the Public Service (see Box 1.2) in 2003. Moreover, a set of practical tools (OECD, 2005) was designed to assist governments putting conflict-of-interest and integrity policies into daily practice. In reviewing progress made in implementing the 2003 Recommendation, post-public employment conflict of interest and lobbying were identified as emerging issues that needed to be addressed by the OECD because there had been no comparative studies of post-public employment policies and practices.

Box 1.2. **OECD Guidelines for Managing Conflict of Interest in the Public Service**

The OECD Guidelines for Managing Conflict of Interest in the Public Service help policy makers review and modernise existing conflict-of-interest policy and practice for public officials, including public servants, civil servants, employees and public office holders. The Guidelines reflect, in particular, policies and practices that have proved effective in OECD countries, and are designed to:

- help government institutions and agencies to develop an effective conflict-of-interest policy that fosters public confidence in their integrity, and the integrity of public officials and public decision making;
- create a practical framework of reference for reviewing existing solutions and modernising mechanisms in line with good practices in OECD countries;
- promote a public service culture where conflicts of interest are properly identified and resolved or managed, in an appropriately transparent and timely way, without unduly inhibiting the effectiveness and efficiency of the public organisations concerned;
- support partnerships between the public sector and the business and non-profit sectors, in accordance with clear public standards defining the parties' responsibilities for integrity.

The Guidelines provide a suite of core principles, policy frameworks, institutional strategies and management tools for managing conflict of interest, arranged in three sections:

- managing conflicts of interest: aims, approach, definitions and principles;
- developing the policy framework;
- implementing the policy framework.

Source: OECD (2004), *Managing Conflict of Interest in the Public Service: OECD Guidelines and Country Experiences*, OECD, Paris.

A significant concern about post-public employment offences, like conflict of interest in general, is that they could significantly undermine public trust in government. In democratic societies, potential decline of citizens' trust in public institutions and confidence in public decision making justify strong and concerted actions to promote good public governance. The development and implementation of effective measures to prevent breaches to integrity, such as post-public employment offences, can help maintain or re-establish public confidence in the integrity of governmental activities.

This task is made more difficult by an increased concern about post-public employment, namely the citizens' perception that certain public sector reforms have brought some public officials into unduly cosy relationships with business and non-profit organisations and created grey areas with risks to integrity. New approaches to public sector management, including the substantial expansion of public-private partnerships, sponsorship, privatisation, concession and contracting out arrangements, have resulted in close interactions with the private sector and increased opportunities for conflict-of-interest situations, especially those related to post-employment of public officials. Moreover, urging public servants to treat citizens as "customers" or "clients" may prompt some of them to provide "special service" in the hope of improving their post-public employment prospects.

Last but not least, making use of insider information and improperly employing formal public officials during their "cooling-off" period may also result in an "unfair advantage" over competitors and could endanger competition in the private sector.

As an example, Box 1.3 presents important reasons why the public should pay more attention to post-public employment, as found by the U.S. Revolving Door Working Group.

Public sector career: Changing patterns

Emerging concerns about post-public employment are also related to the ongoing changes in the career patterns of public servants who leave traditional lifelong public service careers. In a growing number of countries, the traditional notion of career public service in the sense of security of tenure has diminished or disappeared as a result of substantial public sector reforms as well as staff cutbacks associated with government downsizing (OECD, 2008). The decrease in public servants' perception of their probable job security encourages them to pay much more attention to employment opportunities outside the public sector.

At the same time, encouraged by many government initiatives to develop skills and acquire broader knowledge and experiences, the concept of a modern career increasingly includes employment in both the public and private sectors. Employees are moving much more frequently between public and private sector jobs, both as a normal aspect of their working lives and, in some jurisdictions, as part of government-sponsored exchange programmes. This means that more and more public servants will be open and attentive to emerging private-sector job opportunities in order to develop new skills and obtain unique experiences, as well as to boost their career prospects. However, many of them do not expect to permanently leave the public sector. On the

Box 1.3. Six reasons for paying more attention to personnel movement between the private and public sectors

The report of the Revolving Door Working Group in the United States, "A Matter of Trust: How the Revolving Door Undermines Public Confidence in Government – and What to Do About It", reviewed issues related to movement between the federal government and the private sector and listed six important reasons why the public should pay more attention to the "revolving door" phenomenon:

1. It can provide a vehicle for public servants to use their office for personal or private gain at the expense of the American taxpayer.
2. The revolving door phenomenon casts grave doubts on the integrity of official actions and legislation. A member of Congress or a government employee could well be influenced in his or her official actions by promises of a future high-paying job from a business that has a pecuniary interest in the official's actions while in government. Even if the official is not unduly influenced by promises of future employment, the appearance of undue influence itself casts aspersions on the integrity of the federal government.
3. It can provide some government contractors with unfair advantages over their competitors, due to insider knowledge that can be used to the benefit of the contractor, and potentially to the detriment of the public interest.
4. The former employee may have privileged access to government officials. Tapping into a closed network friends and colleagues built while in office, a government employee-turned lobbyist may well have access to power brokers not available to others. In some cases, these networks could involve prior obligations and favours. Former members of Congress even retain privileged access to the Congressional gym, dining hall and floors of Congress.
5. It has resulted in a highly complex but ultimately ineffective framework of ethics and conflict-of-interest regulations. Enforcing those regulations has become a virtual industry within the government, costing significant resources but rarely resulting in sanctions or convictions of those accused of violating the rules. As a result, ethics rules offer little or no deterrent to those who might violate the public trust.
6. The appearance of impropriety exacerbates public distrust in government, ultimately causing a decline in civic participation. It also demoralises honest government workers who do not use their government jobs as a stepping stone to lucrative employment government contractors or lobbying firms.

Source: Revolving Door Working Group (2005), "A Matter of Trust: How the Revolving Door Undermines Public Confidence in Government – and What to Do About It", *www.revolvingdoor.info.*

contrary, they intend to return to the public sector after working for a few years in the private sector: this in itself can raise new possibilities for conflict-of-interest situations.

Post-employment restrictions *versus* employment freedom: Striking a balance

There is a clear need to better identify, prevent and manage the more frequent post-public employment problems that result from increased personnel movement between the public and private sectors. Equally important, however, is the need to strike an appropriate balance between promoting integrity (defined here as "the proper use of funds, resources, assets, and powers, for the official purposes for which they are intended to be used" [OECD, 2005, p. 7]) in the public sector through strict prohibitions and restrictions in the post-public employment system on the one hand, and preserving a reasonable measure of employment freedom for current and former public officials on the other.

Given the increasing competition between the public and private sectors for knowledge workers and the increasing motivation of, and need for, public servants to enhance their skills and knowledge through private sector experience, governments must be careful to strike an adequate balance and not to impose post-public employment prohibitions and restrictions that are unduly stringent. Consequently, prohibitions and restrictions may be considered as temporary solutions, and policy makers might seek to establish reasonable time limits – for example in the form of a "cooling-off" period – tailored to the gravity of actual and potential risks.

Structure and scope

Post-public employment offences involve activities primarily by former rather than current public officials. In some countries post-public employment is described as "post-office employment" or "post-separation employment". While politicians are not included in the term public "employees", the term post-public employment is applied in common usage to cover both politicians and public servants. The term "public officials" is used throughout this book to include both public servants and politicians either elected or appointed.

Based on OECD country experiences, the following chapters review the relevant aspects of practice and components of a comprehensive framework for preventing conflict of interest in post-public employment. Specifically, it will:

- outline the concerns driving the policy review and update;
- analyse current approaches and existing standards (*e.g.* prohibitions and restrictions) for preventing conflict of interest in post-public employment;

- review existing solutions – for example by examining their strengths and weaknesses – to measure the effectiveness of arrangements for implementing and enforcing post-public employment prohibitions and restrictions, in particular the procedures, incentives and sanctions.

Chapter 2 explains the nature and implications of five major post-public employment problem areas. Chapters 3 and 4 examine the management of these problems. Chapter 3 provides principles for managing post-public employment problems and Chapter 4 provides a framework of post-public employment guidelines for developing an effective post-public employment system that includes instruments, procedures and structures in the form of policies and practices to manage post-public employment conflict of interest.[2] Chapter 4 also explains the pillars of the good practice framework for implementing the principles and presents examples of selected good practice. The good practices discuss topics such as selecting implementation instruments, covering risk and enforcing sanctions.

Notes

1. "Strengthening Trust in Government: What Role for Government in the 21st Century?" was the central theme of the ministerial meeting of the OECD Public Governance Committee in 2005 in Rotterdam, Netherlands. Further details on the meeting are available at *www.modernisinggovernment.com*.
2. Post-employment policies and practices are an essential part of the integrity framework in public organisations, as outlined in *Towards a Sound Integrity Framework: Instruments, Mechanisms, Actors and Conditions for Implementation*, OECD, GOV/PGC/GF(2009)1.

Bibliography

Institut CSA (2006), *Les Français et la Fonction publique*, Sondage de l'Institut CSA, February.

OECD (2004), *Managing Conflict of Interest in the Public Service: OECD Guidelines and Country Experiences*, OECD, Paris.

OECD (2005), *Managing Conflict of Interest in the Public Sector: A Toolkit*, OECD, Paris.

OECD (2006), *Towards More and Better-Paid Jobs: A Reassessment of the OECD Jobs Strategy*, OECD, Paris.

OECD (2008), *The State of the Public Service*, OECD, Paris.

OECD (2009), *Towards a Sound Integrity Framework: Instruments, Mechanisms, Actors and Conditions for Implementation*, OECD, Paris, GOV/PGC/GF(2009)1.

Revolving Door Working Group (2005), "A Matter of Trust: How the Revolving Door Undermines Public Confidence in Government – and What to Do About It", *www.revolvingdoor.info*.

Post-Public Employment
Good Practices for Preventing Conflict of Interest

Chapter 2

Post-public employment problem areas

This chapter reviews major types of post-public employment offences. It begins by examining a problem area that arises before the official actually leaves government: seeking future employment outside the public service. Problem areas involving public officials after they have left office include: conducting post-employment lobbying back to government institutions; switching sides in the same process; or using insider information. The chapter reviews the problem resulting from the re-employment or re-engagement of former officials by public organisations, for example, to do the same tasks they performed in the private or non-profit sectors.

Seeking future employment

While individuals are still working for public organisations and expected to promote the public interest, they can take measures to improve their future employment prospects outside the public sector. They can give preferential treatment, in such forms as contracts, grants, subsidies or lax rule enforcement, to outside organisations. This offence is often described as "going soft" on particular clients in the performance of one's official responsibilities. Officials performing regulatory roles (*e.g.* bank and assurance, environmental protection, workplace safety, police) are in an especially good position to take advantage of their public office in this fashion. Involvement in this offence is facilitated by the well-known phenomenon of "regulatory capture" according to which regulatory officials whose mandate is to seek the public interest end up favouring the interests of those being regulated – and in some cases favouring their own interests in future employment over their official duties.

Offering reward in the form of a post-employment job can often occur in such a subtle way that a public official's colleagues may not suspect wrongdoing or, if they do, are unable to prove it. What appears to be special treatment for a client is often difficult to distinguish from what is simply good service. However, even suspicion of rewarding favourable decisions in the past – in particular in public procurement, including the tendering or contract management stage, or in privatisation – which may have substantially benefited a prospective employer could similarly endanger trust in public decision making.

Consequently, appropriate care must be taken to control bias through ensuring that public officials' emphasis on customer-centred or client-centred service, pursued in part through their close contacts with employees in private and non-profit organisations, does not gradually develop into unduly favourable treatment. Commission of this offence is often evidenced by the granting of treatment to certain clients that is not fairly and equitably available to all clients.

Post-public employment lobbying

Lobbying is a worldwide practice that can provide policy makers with invaluable insight and data for more informed decision making. Consequently, in modern democracies, lobbying politicians and public servants to influence the development and implementation of public policies and programmes is considered legitimate. However, lobbying is often perceived negatively across the globe, as giving special advantages to vocal vested interests. Concerns that negotiations carried out behind closed doors could override the interests of the whole community have pushed lobbying to the political agenda in many societies.

It is increasingly acknowledged that former public officials with knowledge and access to other public officials are an asset in the lobbyists' world. Lobbying government by former public officials is the form of post-public employment problem most highlighted by the media. Improper conduct, even corrupt activities by some lobbyists, especially in respect of government decisions regarding the awarding of contracts, grants and subsidies has increased public concern and driven decision makers to establish or strengthen specific restrictions. These restrictions include adequate "cooling-off" periods during which former public officials are not to lobby back their former government organisations. However, only a few OECD countries and non-members have responded to this concern by adopting rules and disclosure procedures for lobbyists that are designed to prevent and control possible misconduct by requesting increased transparency and accountability in lobbying (*e.g.* through registration and disclosure by lobbyists) (OECD, 2009c).

There is a close connection between lobbying and conflict of interest, particularly post-public employment conflict of interest. A post-public employment problem arises when persons who have left government seek to lobby their former employer on behalf of themselves or their new employer. Their former government colleagues may feel pressured or obliged to grant them preferential treatment. This treatment can take such forms as privileged access to decision makers, private or secret consultations, improper access to information and even biased decisions. These special opportunities are not available to the lobbyist's competitors – if the lobbyist is running his or her own business – or to the competitors of the lobbyist's new employer. As a result, fairness and transparency in government decision making come into question.

Moreover, post-employment lobbying back to former government institutions is related to the previous offence: public officials who are contemplating leaving the public sector to become lobbyists may be tempted to give preferential treatment to potential employers in the private and not-for-profit sectors.

As explained in the next section, a common remedy in such cases is the imposition of a cooling-off period – a designated period of time during which former public officials cannot accept employment with certain private sector organisations or cannot represent any entity in dealings with specified parts of the government where those representations are likely to constitute a real or apparent conflict of interest. For many public servants who have left government, it may be adequate to restrict their access to their former departments or agencies, but for senior officials, especially ministers with extensive contacts, information and influence, government-wide prohibitions may be considered necessary. Furthermore, restrictions may also prohibit using information obtained during public office that has been classified as "confidential" until that information loses its classification or is otherwise disclosed by the government.

Switching sides

In the normal course of government operations, there are many disputes between public officials and non-governmental actors over such matters as compliance with regulations, the adjudication of claims, and the awarding of contracts, grants and subsidies. A post-public employment problem arises when former public officials "switch sides", that is, when they represent themselves or their new employer to government in an ongoing procedure or negotiation on a contentious issue for which they had responsibility when they worked for the public sector.

The following practical example can highlight the concerns related to the problem: a revenue official dealing with a tax dispute with a private firm could leave his or her office and then represent that firm's side against the government in the same dispute. Many countries employ strict rules against switching sides. For example, in Canada, no former public office holder is permitted to "act for or on behalf of any person or organisation in connection with any specific proceeding, transaction, negotiation or case to which the Crown is a party and with respect to which the former public office holder had acted for, or provided advice to, the Crown" (Canada, 2006).

Switching sides draws attention to an evident form of post-public employment problem. This offence is similar to, but narrower than, the lobbying problem discussed above. Similarly to lobbying, this problem is handled by imposing a cooling-off period during which former public officials are prohibited from switching sides. However, the applied timeframe is linked to the life of the matter; therefore the ban remains valid until the matter is completed (a life of the matter restriction).

Using insider information

Collecting, analysing and processing information is a fundamental activity of governments and a crucial aspect of public decision making. All democratic governments impose restrictions on public officials' use of confidential information, often by such means as requiring officials to take an oath of office and secrecy. In addition, officials' use of confidential information for personal or private benefit is widely viewed as a conflict-of-interest issue.

A post-public employment conflict of interest arises when public officials who leave government take unfair advantage of confidential information that they acquired while in government to benefit themselves or their new employer. The broad term "insider information" is commonly used to refer not only to information that is formally classified as confidential but also to information to which public officials have access by virtue of their official position and which has not been made available to the general public.

OECD countries in general prohibit the misuse of insider information: for example in Canada, a former public officeholder is prohibited from giving "advice to his or her client, business associate or employer using information that was obtained in his or her capacity as a public office holder and is not available to the public" (Canada, 2006).

Another example is provided in Box 2.1, in which Norway developed the Post-Employment Guidelines for the Public Service in 2005 out of a need to protect internal information, protect other organisations' trade secrets and safeguard public confidence in the public service.

Box 2.1. **Norway: Concerns leading to the development of the Post-Employment Guidelines for the Public Service**

Although Norwegian State administrative agencies do not regularly operate in a competitive market, they may have justifiable needs for post-public employment clauses in employee contracts, similarly to private sector companies. Concerns related to post-public employment reached the Parliament which debated them in 2000-01. Following the recommendations of the Parliament, the Post-Employment Guidelines for the Public Service were developed for the following reasons:

- The need to protect internal information: The State must seek to prevent other organisations from gaining knowledge about an administrative agency's strategy and plans, e.g. on the formulation of policy and regulations. Such knowledge could result in illegal competitive advantage.
- The need to protect other organisations' trade secrets: The State must seek to prevent an organisation from gaining access to confidential information about other organisations, including trade secrets, etc. Such knowledge could also result in illegal competitive advantage.
- The need to safeguard public confidence in the public service: State administrative agencies must seek to prevent suspicions that a civil servant has taken advantage of his or her position to gain special advantages for an organisation. Such suspicions could weaken public confidence in the integrity and impartiality of the administration.

These concerns may be considered to justify preventive actions such as "temporary disqualification" and/or "abstinence from involvement in certain cases".

Source: Norway (2005a), "Post-Employment Guidelines for the Public Service", July; Norway (2005b), "Post-Employment Guidelines for Politicians", November.

In practice, governments have to distinguish between former officials' misuse of insider information and their legitimate use of knowledge and skills gained from their work experience in government. Moreover, achieving an appropriate balance between counter measures against misuse of insider information and providing a reasonable employment freedom for current and former public officials is necessary if governments want to continue to attract experienced knowledge workers.

The imposition of a cooling-off period, previously noted as a means of managing the problems of post-public employment lobbying and switching sides, can also be applied to prevent misuse of insider information because that information tends to have a limited "shelf life". This prohibition generally remains valid until the insider information becomes unclassified or is made public.

Re-engaging or re-employing former officials

A final type of post-public employment problem arises when former public officials are re-engaged by public organisations to do substantially the same work that they did when they were employed there. Public officials are sometimes re-engaged by being brought back to public organisations as consultants on contracts to perform the same tasks they did previously. Given the increasing mobility of individuals between the public and private sectors and the specific expertise of former officials, the magnitude of this problem is likely to increase.

Clearly, there are circumstances in which such arrangements are appropriate and necessary. A public servant, for example, may leave at the normal retirement age but then can be hired back on a contract basis – even at a higher pay level – because of a pressing need for his or her expertise and the public organisation's inability to find an adequate replacement.

There is somewhat less concern about re-engagement or re-employment if a former official is hired to work in a part of the public sector that is not directly connected with his or her former job. However, conflict of interest may appear when former public servants are engaged on a contractual basis to provide services for a public organisation they worked for before, in particular when they are re-hired or engaged on a contractual basis for the same task. They can be seen as benefitting from connections to their former colleagues. Consequently, an appropriately competitive and transparent hiring process for engaging former colleagues is critical to prevent potential or actual conflict of interest specifically, and ensure fairness of the hiring process, generally.

Bibliography

Canada (2006), "Conflict of Interest Act", December, Sec. 34(1).

OECD (2009c), *Lobbyists, Government and Public Trust: Increasing Transparency Through Legislation*, OECD, Paris.

OECD (2009d), *Self-Regulation and Regulation of the Lobbying Profession*, OECD GOV/PGC/GF(2009)5.

Norway (2005a), "Post-Employment Guidelines for the Public Service", July.

Norway (2005b), "Post-Employment Guidelines for Politicians", November.

Chapter 3

Principles for managing post-public employment problems

This chapter presents a set of principles for preventing and managing the post-public employment problems reviewed in the previous chapter. This chapter outlines comprehensive guidelines and alternative solutions that policy makers can consider as they work to prevent and manage post-public employment conflict of interest and to counter probable offences.

Introduction

Governments experience particular challenges as they work to develop effective legal frameworks, policies and practices to prevent and manage post-public employment problems as such problems generally arise when former public officials have moved beyond the control of government, having left the public sector.

Experience shows that there is no one best approach to fostering integrity. This is also true when dealing with post-public employment problems: each country needs to develop its own post-public employment system for dealing with its specific and particular post-public employment problems as well as anticipate emerging issues. Consequently, each country's post-public employment system must be tailored to the particular problems it faces and to the demands of its political, legal and administrative systems.

The relative importance of the five problem areas – examined in Chapter 2 – varies both within a single public sector and from one country to another. However, it is commonly thought that managing and monitoring post-public employment offences is more difficult than managing other types of conflict of interest as restrictions can be imposed much more easily on current officials than on former ones. Therefore, alternative solutions – such as incentives to encourage voluntary compliance with high standards of integrity – are more important in managing post-public employment problems than other conflict-of-interest situations.

Designing the Post-Public Employment Principles

This section introduces the Principles for Managing Post-Public Employment Conflict of Interest in the Public Service – hereafter referred to as the Post-Public Employment Principles – which identify essential components of a comprehensive post-public employment system.

The Post-Public Employment Principles were designed to provide a point of reference against which policy makers and managers in public sector organisations can assess the strengths and deficiencies of current post-public employment systems in light of their existing and anticipated needs. As explained later, policy makers and agency managers can choose those principles that best meet their specific requirements and then implement them through appropriate regulations, policies and practices.

The Post-Public Employment Principles are fundamentally based on the problem areas reviewed in Chapter 2 and on the restrictions and prohibitions on post-public employment examined in the OECD survey on "Avoiding Conflict of Interest in Post-public Employment" (OECD, 2006). The Post-Public Employment Principles have been developed on the basis of the core principles contained in the OECD Guidelines for Managing Conflict of Interest in the Public Service (OECD, 2004) (hereafter referred to as the OECD Conflict of Interest Guidelines) that provide a common framework for managing conflict-of-interest situations in the public service.

Several of the principles shown under the four core principles of the OECD Conflict of Interest Guidelines pertain to the post-public employment issue, generally speaking. For example, under "Supporting transparency and scrutiny" a principle notes that "[p]ublic officials' private interests and affiliations that could compromise the disinterested performance of public duties should be disclosed appropriately, to enable adequate control and management of a resolution." One specific principle, under "Serving the public interest", addresses directly the post-public employment issue by stating that "[p]ublic officials are expected not to take improper advantage of a public office or official position which they held previously, including privileged information obtained in that position, especially when seeking employment or appointment after leaving public office."

Box 3.1 lists the principles included in the OECD Conflict of Interest Guidelines under the following core principles:

- serving the public interest;
- supporting transparency and scrutiny;
- promoting individual responsibility and personal example;
- engendering an organisational culture which is intolerant of conflicts of interest.

While the Post-Public Employment Principles are tailored to meet the specific challenges posed by post-public employment problems, they share the spirit and intent of the broader OECD Conflict of Interest Guidelines. The Post-Public Employment Principles provide a general framework that can be tailored by policy makers and managers to fit their specific public sector or agency context and needs.

The Post-Public Employment Principles are grouped into four functional categories:

1. The first category involves problems that arise primarily while officials are **still working in the public sector** (Principles 1-5).
2. The second category entails problems that arise primarily **after officials leave government** (Principles 6-9).
3. The third category focuses on the duty of current officials to **avoid preferential treatment** of former public officials (Principles 10-12).

Box 3.1. **OECD Principles for Managing Conflict of Interest**

The OECD Guidelines for Managing Conflict of Interest in the Public Service contain the following Principles that public officials are expected to observe when dealing with conflict of interest matters in order to promote integrity in the performance of official duties and responsibilities.

Serving the public interest

- Public officials should make decisions and provide advice on the basis of the relevant law and policy, and the merits of each case, without regard for personal gain (*i.e.* be "disinterested"). The integrity of official decision making, in particular in the application of policy to individual cases, should not be prejudiced by the religious, professional, party-political, ethnic, family, or other personal preferences or alignments of the decision-maker.
- Public officials should dispose of, or restrict the operation of, private interests that could compromise official decisions in which they participate. Where this is not feasible, a public official should abstain from involvement in official decisions which could be compromised by their private-capacity interests and affiliations.
- Public officials should avoid private-capacity action which could derive an improper advantage from "inside information" obtained in the course of official duties, where the information is not generally available to the public, and are required not to misuse their position and government resources for private gain.
- Public officials should not seek or accept any form of improper benefit in expectation of influencing the performance or non-performance of official duties or functions.
- Public officials are expected not to take improper advantage of a public office or official position which they held previously, including privileged information obtained in that position, especially when seeking employment or appointment after leaving public office.

Supporting transparency and scrutiny

- Public officials and public organisations are expected to act in a manner that will bear the closest public scrutiny. This obligation is not fully discharged simply by acting within the letter of the law; it also entails respecting broader public service values such as disinterestedness, impartiality and integrity.
- Public officials private interests and affiliations that could compromise the disinterested performance of public duties should be disclosed appropriately, to enable adequate control and management of a resolution.
- Public organisations and officials should ensure consistency and an appropriate degree of openness in the process of resolving or managing a conflict of interest situation.
- Public officials and public organisations should promote scrutiny of their management of conflict-of-interest situations, within the applicable legal framework.

Box 3.1. **OECD Principles for Managing Conflict of Interest** *(cont.)*

Promoting individual responsibility and personal example

- Public officials are expected to act at all times so that their integrity serves an example to other public officials and the public.
- Public officials should accept responsibility for arranging their private-capacity affairs, as far as reasonably possible, so as to prevent conflicts of interest arising on appointment to public office and thereafter.
- Public officials should accept responsibility for identifying and resolving conflicts in favour of the public interest when a conflict does arise.
- Public officials and public organisations are expected to demonstrate their commitment to integrity and professionalism through their application of effective conflict-of-interest policy and practice.

Engendering an organisational culture which is intolerant of conflicts of interest

- Public organisations should provide and implement adequate management policies, processes, and practices in the working environment to encourage the effective control and management of conflict-of-interest situations.
- Organisational practices should encourage public officials to disclose and discuss conflict-of-interest matters, and provide reasonable measures to protect disclosures from misuse by others.
- Public organisations should create and sustain a culture of open communication and dialogue concerning integrity and its promotion.
- Public organisations should provide guidance and training to promote understanding and dynamic evolution of the public organisation's established rules and practices, and their application to the working environment.

Source: OECD (2004), *Managing Conflict of Interest in the Public Service: OECD Guidelines and Country Experiences*, OECD, Paris

4. Finally, Principle 13 involves non-governmental employers and underlines the **responsibility of private firms and non-profit organisations to avoid post-public employment problems** when employing former public officials.

Some of these principles – for example "prohibiting the use of insider information" – are aimed at a particular problem area whereas others, such as "announcing an official's intention to leave the public sector", pertain to more than one problem area. Thus, each problem area should be carefully assessed in terms of the relevant principles that could prove useful in preventing, managing, monitoring and enforcing it.

Post-Public Employment Principles

The Principles for Managing Post-Public Employment Conflict of Interest in the Public Service (the Post-Public Employment Principles) organise essential components of a post-public employment system within a comprehensive and coherent structure. The Principles provide a point of reference against which policy makers and managers in public sector organisations can review the strengths and weaknesses of their current post-public employment system and modernise it in light of their specific context, including existing needs and anticipated problems.

Problems arising primarily while officials are still working in government

1. Public officials should not enhance their future employment prospects in the private and non-profit sectors by giving preferential treatment to potential employers.
2. Public officials should, in a timely manner, disclose their seeking or negotiating of employment and offers of employment that could constitute a conflict of interest.
3. Public officials should, in a timely manner, disclose their intention to seek and negotiate employment and the acceptance of an offer of employment in the private and non-profit sectors that could constitute a conflict of interest.
4. Public officials, who have decided to take up employment in the private and non-profit sectors, should, where feasible, be excused from current duties that could constitute a conflict of interest with their likely responsibilities to their future employer.
5. Before leaving the public sector, public officials who are in a position to become involved in a conflict of interest should have an exit interview with the appropriate authority to examine possible conflict-of-interest situations and, if necessary, determine appropriate measures for remedy.

Problems arising primarily after public officials have left government

6. Public officials should not use confidential or other "insider" information after they leave the public sector.
7. Public officials who leave the public sector should be restricted in their efforts to lobby their former subordinates and colleagues in the public sector. An appropriate subject matter limit, time limit or "cooling-off" period may be imposed.
8. The post-public employment system should take into consideration appropriate measures to prevent and manage conflict of interest when public officials accept appointments to entities with which the officials had

significant official dealings before they left the public sector. An appropriate subject matter limit, time limit or cooling-off period may be required.

9. Public officials should be prohibited from "switching sides" and representing their new employer in an ongoing procedure on a contentious issue for which they had responsibility before they left the public sector.

Duties of current officials in dealing with former public officials

10. Current public officials should be prohibited from granting preferential treatment, special access or privileged information to anyone, including former officials.
11. Current public officials who engage former public officials on a contractual basis to do essentially the same job as the former officials performed when they worked in a public organisation should ensure that the hiring process has been appropriately competitive and transparent.
12. The post-public employment system should give consideration on how to handle redundancy payments received by former public officials when they are re-employed.

Responsibilities of organisations that employ former public officials

13. Private firms and non-profit organisations should be restricted in using or encouraging officials who are seeking to leave or who have left government to engage in activities that are prohibited by law or regulation.

Bibliography

OECD (2004), *Managing Conflict of Interest in the Public Service: OECD Guidelines and Country Experiences*, OECD, Paris, pp. 21-37.

OECD (2006), "Avoiding Conflict of Interest in Post-public Employment: Comparative Overview of Prohibitions, Restrictions and Implementing Measures in OECD Countries", OECD unclassified document, GOV/PGC/ETH(2006)3, *www.olis.oecd.org/olis/2006doc.nsf/LinkToFrench/NT0000B9CE/$FILE/JT00197267.PDF*.

Chapter 4

Implementing the Post-Public Employment Principles: A good practice framework

This chapter introduces the Post-Public Employment Good Practice Framework and discusses its key pillars, through which the Post-Public Employment Principles can be implemented. The framework also includes elements of good practice. These concrete examples from various jurisdictions provide policy makers and managers with alternative options and benchmarks. Reviewed good practices include the selection of implementation mechanisms, the coverage of risk areas and enforcement of sanctions.

Introduction

It may not be immediately evident how to implement the Post-Public Employment Principles set out in Chapter 3. Policy makers and managers may wish to start by systematically examining to what extent their existing post-public employment measures can meet the requirements outlined by the principles. The Post-Public Employment Good Practice Framework (hereafter referred to as the "Good Practice Framework"), described in this chapter, provides a range of measures that could be considered for comprehensive, effective and transparent implementation of the principles. The framework contains the key policies and practices to prevent, manage and control post-public employment conflict of interest.

The Good Practice Framework can be used to assess the current state of post-public employment systems both by managers in individual public sector organisations and by policy makers at the national and sub-national levels on a comparative basis.

An effective post-public employment system encompasses the following key pillars and characteristics:

1. The post-public employment system contains the instrument(s) needed to deal effectively with its current and anticipated post-public employment problems and emerging concerns.
2. The post-public employment instrument(s) is (are) linked, where feasible, with instrument(s) dealing with conflict of interest in the public sector and with the overall values and integrity framework.
3. The post-public employment system covers all of the entities for which post-public employment is a real or potential problem, and meets the distinctive needs of each entity.
4. The post-public employment system covers all of the important risk areas for post-public employment conflict of interest.
5. The restrictions, in particular the length of time limits imposed on the activities of former public officials, are proportionate to the gravity of the post-public employment conflict of interest threat that the officials pose.
6. The restrictions and prohibitions contained in the post-public employment system are effectively communicated to all affected parties.

7. The authorities, procedures and criteria for making approval decisions in individual post-public employment cases, as well as for appeals against these decisions, are transparent and effective.
8. The enforcement sanctions for post-public employment offences are clear and proportional, and are timely, consistently and equitably applied.
9. The effectiveness of the policies and practices contained in each post-public employment system is assessed regularly and, where appropriate, is updated and adjusted to emerging concerns.

In the following sections, each of the components of the Good Practice Framework are discussed. References to elements of good practice – drawn from OECD countries that are reported (in research results) or reputed (by experts in the field) to work well – illustrate available policy options and benchmarks. Careful choice among available instruments is critical to effectively manage post-public employment. Consequently, more details on elements of good practices are highlighted to provide further information on the context. However, policy makers and managers should carefully integrate post-public employment systems in the broader Integrity Framework and ensure a balance with the need to provide sufficient employment freedom to former public officials. Post-public employment prohibitions and restrictions should not discourage well-qualified persons from entering the public sector or unduly reducing their employment prospects after they leave public organisations.

Implementation instruments

1. The post-public employment system contains the instrument(s) needed to deal effectively with its current and anticipated post-public employment problems and emerging concerns.

Governments are generally aware of potential risks to integrity in post-public employment and the vast majority of OECD countries set out prohibitions and restrictions to avoid conflict of interest in post-public employment (OECD, 2006a). In order to maintain trust in government and public decision making, post-public employment systems prohibit the use of insider information and discourage the inappropriate use of personal influence, *e.g.* to avoid suspicion of having made decisions which may have benefited a prospective employer (Figure 4.1).

Post-public employment prohibitions and restrictions predominantly focus on officials leaving public office. However, a few countries, *e.g.* France and the United States, can impose restrictions on the criminal code for the potential or new employer of former public officials.

According to the formal sources, a variety of instruments has been used for preventing and managing post-public employment conflict of interest, including primary legislation as the most common instrument, followed by codes of

Figure 4.1. **Aims of prohibitions and restrictions**

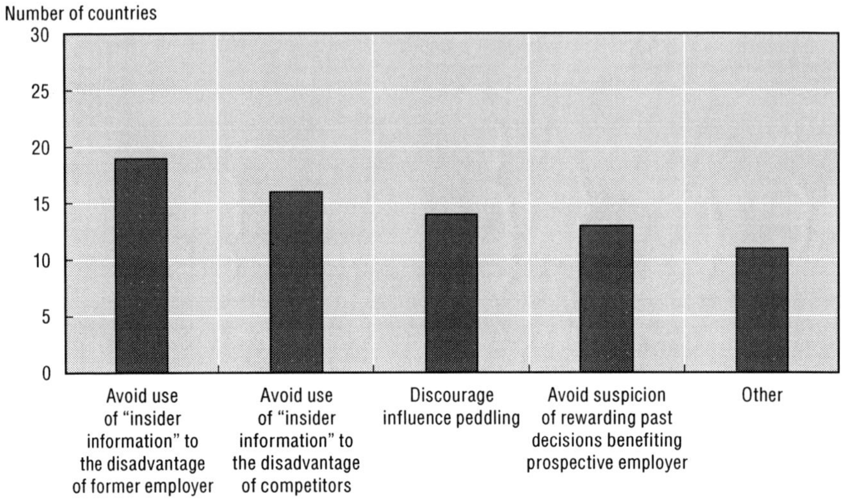

Source: OECD (2006).

conduct, secondary legislation, other legal documents and non-legal documents. Each category of instruments is examined briefly in the following sections.

Primary legislation

The principal source of post-public employment prohibitions and restrictions is primary legislation. Primary legislation dealing with post-public employment conflict of interest, like that which deals with conflict of interest in general, can take various forms, including:

- General laws on civil and public service or the public administration: for example, the General Statute of Officials in Belgium and France; the Acts on Federal Civil Servants in Austria and Germany; the Act on Civil Service in the Slovak Republic, the National Public Service Act in Japan; and the Public Administration Act in Denmark.
- Laws on specific groups of public officials: for example, the Act on the Legal Status of Soldiers in Germany, and the Act on Judges in Austria as well as electoral codes in France and Ireland.
- Criminal codes: for example, in Denmark and the United States.

Some countries enacted acts specifically aimed at setting standards of integrity that also include provisions on post-public employment, such as:

- Canada's Federal Accountability Act toughened the Lobbyist Registration Act by introducing a five-year ban on lobbying for ministers, ministerial staffers and senior public servants;
- Turkey's Law on Prohibitions of Post-public Employment (Law No. 2531);

- Poland's Limitation on Conducting Business Activity by Persons Performing Public Functions Act (1997);
- Ireland's Ethics in Public Office Act (1995) and the Standards in Public Office Act (2001);
- Spain's Act on Conflict of Interest approved in May 2006 that replaced the 1995 Law on Incompatibilities of High-Ranking Public Officials.

An attractive feature of primary legislation is that it provides strict standards for sanction and can, therefore, be a more effective deterrent than other instruments. However, while primary legislation may be a powerful deterrent to post-public employment conflict of interest, it can also be a strong disincentive to prospective public officials who may view these prohibitions and constraints as unduly restrictive of their rights.

Secondary legislation

Secondary legislation – in the form of **directives, rules, regulations and decrees** – is usually authorised by, and directly related to, a piece of primary legislation in order to provide further specificities. Secondary legislation would, for example, elaborate on the provisions of a statute dealing with conflict of interest in general, or with post-public employment conflict of interest in particular. In Japan, primary legislation in the form of the National Public Service Act is supplemented by secondary legislation in the form of the rules of the National Personnel Authority. Secondary legislation is generally issued by the central organisation in charge of the implementation of the post-public employment restrictions, *e.g.* the National Personnel Authority in Japan or the Federal Ministry of Defence in Germany that issued the Ordinance of 2 September 2002.

Secondary legislation enhances the deterrent value of primary legislation by giving greater specificity to its application and enforcement. An advantage of using secondary legislation to implement primary legislation is that it can be amended relatively easily to take account of desirable changes in a country's post-public employment system.

Box 4.1 presents Portugal's use of secondary legislation to address post-public employment.

Other legal instruments

Other legal instruments can take a variety of forms, including **orders, circulars, collective agreements and contracts**. They are potentially useful in dealing with specific post-public employment problem areas where there are objections to legislative solutions.

Box 4.1. Portugal: Use of secondary legislation to address post-public employment

Top public officeholders in Portugal have traditionally been prohibited by law to act as an arbitrator or expert in any procedure where the State and other public legal entities are an intervening party during their tenure, and for a one-year period after termination of their functions. Breach of such prohibition results in the annulation of acts committed by higher management officeholders or equivalent level officials.

In addition, a decree on the public manager statute (Decree Law 71/2007, 27 March) proscribes public managers, during the performance of their terms of office, to sign any employment contracts with prospective employers or for the provision of services with companies in the same sector after the termination of their functions. The decree, however, allows exceptions provided by the specific authorisation of the member of the government responsible for the finance area and the member of the government responsible for the relevant sector.

Breach of rules related to incompatibilities and prohibitions by public managers may be sanctioned according to the decree by dismissal that implies not only the termination of the term of office but also releases the obligation to grant any subsidy or compensation due to any termination of functions.

Source: Portuguese response to OECD survey.

Including a clause on post-public employment restrictions in contracts is an emerging trend and a good example of other legal instruments (see Box 4.2). Specific clauses on post-public employment can provide a tailored response to address potential post-employment problems. In addition, a signed contract provides a solid basis for enforcing the prohibitions defined by the clause, *e.g.* in a judicial procedure.

Box 4.2. Australia, New Zealand and Norway: Including post-public employment clauses in contracts

Many agencies in the Australian Public Service include references to their post-public employment rules in contracts with private sector organisations.

New Zealand's employment contracts for chief executives include post-public employment clauses. They prescribe a cooling-off period that limits the paid activities in which they can engage after they leave the State Service.

Norway adopted separate Post-Employment Guidelines for the Public Service and Post-Employment Guidelines for Politicians in 2005 that are only applicable if they are incorporated into the employment contract of a particular employee.

Source: Australian, New Zealand and Norwegian responses to OECD survey.

Codes of conduct

Legislation is often described as "hard law" as opposed to the "soft law" status of codes of conduct. Codes of conduct take a remarkable **variety of forms** and there are, in addition, instruments that are similar to codes of conduct that are described as **codes of ethics**, **statements of values** or **principles.**[1] Several countries include post-public employment provisions in codes of conduct or codes of ethics, including:

- the Slovak Republic's Code of Ethics issued by the Civil Service Office;
- Turkey's bylaw on Codes of Ethics for Public Servants;
- Spain's Code of Good Government;
- Ireland's Civil Service Code of Standards and Behaviour (Sections 20-21).

Some countries, *e.g.* Australia, have both a statement of values and a code of conduct. Politicians and public servants can be covered together by a single code or they can be subject to separate codes. Moreover, the legal status of the instruments can differ for each group, as illustrated in Box 4.3.

Box 4.3. **Australia and Canada: Use of separate codes of conduct for politicians and public servants**

In Australia, post-employment for public servants is covered by the Australian Public Service (APS) Values and Code of Conduct. To assist APS employees in understanding the practical application of the APS Values and Code of Conduct relevant to post-public employment, the APS Values and Code of Conduct in Practice provides a specific chapter on post-separation employment.

For ministerial conduct, the Prime Minister issued Standards of Ministerial Ethics in December 2007 to replace the relevant part of the Prime Minister's Guide on Key Elements of Ministerial Responsibility, last issued in December 1998. This guide did not impose any legal restrictions on ministers' post-public employment activity, but it did provide that "Ministers should not exercise the influence obtained from their public office, or use official information, to gain any improper benefit for themselves or another." The Standards of Ministerial Ethics, however, includes a specific section on "post-ministerial employment" in which:

- "Ministers are required to undertake that, for an 18-month period after ceasing to be a minister, they will not lobby, advocate or have business meetings with members of the government, parliament, public service or defence force on any matters on which they have had official dealings as minister in their last 18 months in office.
- Ministers are also required to undertake that, on leaving office, they will not take personal advantage of information to which they have had access as a minister, where that information is not generally available to the public.
- Ministers shall ensure that their personal conduct is consistent with the dignity, reputation and integrity of the Parliament" (Australian Government, 2007).

Box 4.3. **Australia and Canada: Use of separate codes of conduct for politicians and public servants** *(cont.)*

In addition to ministers, the Lobbying Code of Conduct, released on 13 May 2008, places restrictions on former members of the APS senior executive service not to "engage in lobbying activities for a 12 month period on any matters on which they have had official dealings as public servants over the last 12 months".

In Canada, the post-public employment activities of political executives and the administrative heads of departments are covered by the 2006 Conflict of Interest Act to which compliance is a condition of employment. Moreover, the Conflict of Interest and Post-employment Code for Public Office Holders* includes post-public employment compliance measures. In addition, the House of Commons (the lower house of Parliament) and the Senate (the upper house) each have a separate code of conduct for their members.

Public servants are covered by the post-public employment provisions of the Values and Ethics Code for the Public Service. This instrument is defined as a policy; compliance with its provisions is a condition of employment for most public servants.

* The Conflict of Interest and Post-employment Code for Public Office Holders can be consulted at *www.parl.gc.ca/ciec%1eccie/en/archives/ethics_commissioner/conflicts/tcp_2006.asp.*

Source: APS Values and Code of Conduct in Practice, Standards of Ministerial Ethics, Lobbying Code of Conduct, Australia; Conflict of Interest Act, Conflict of Interest and Post-employment Code for Public Office Holders, Values and Ethics Code for the Public Service, Canada.

Codes of conduct can be worded very generally (the Ten Commandments or "principle-based" approach) or they can provide for a wide range of possibilities in detail (the Justinian Code or the "rule-based" approach). Some public service codes – or value statements – strike a balance between these two approaches by setting out core public service values (*e.g.* integrity and fairness) as a foundation for prescribing specific principles and rules dealing with several types of conflict-of-interest situations, including post-public employment (see Belgium's Code of Conduct as discussed in the next sections). Finally, some codes provide for their enforcement: for example, the Code of Conduct for the executive branch in the United States has a section on the early stages of merely "seeking" employment which is administratively enforced, whereas restrictions involving actually "negotiating for employment" are governed by criminal statute.

In general, codes of conduct have a weaker deterrent effect than legislation. Codes are likely to be especially ineffective in regulating the post-public employment activities of former officials. Whereas legislation is designed largely to prevent and punish wrongdoing, codes – and value statements – are often designed to foster "right doing" through the use of aspirational and inspirational language, and gently worded admonitions. Codes play a central role in encouraging integrity as opposed to combating corruption. Individual departments – and other public organisations – can use public-sector-wide codes as a framework to develop their own codes, rules and guidelines, especially to deal with specific risk areas and take into consideration the specific context of individual public organisations.

Box 4.4 describes Belgium's Code of Conduct for Federal Public Officials, as an example.

Box 4.4. **Belgium: Code of conduct for federal public officials**

The code of conduct for federal public officials, adopted in August 2007 in Belgium, used the 2003 OECD Recommendation on Guidelines for Managing Conflict of Interest in the Public Service as a basis.

The code of conduct includes measures for post-public employment without regulating them in detail. In particular, federal public officials are obliged to report to their superiors whenever they consider a situation to be a conflict of interest, including when they intend to leave the federal public service. Once public officials have left the public service, their contacts with the federal public service staff cannot benefit from particular favours (*e.g.* insider information received from the administration).

Public officials can have recourse to the Bureau of Ethics and Professional Conduct which is in charge of the coherent implementation of the provisions of the code of conduct. The Bureau provides official advice on the interest and accumulation of mandates cases submitted by federal public officials.

Source: Belgium response to OECD survey.

Non-legal instruments

Non-legal instruments are used less than other instruments for handling post-public employment problems. They take various forms, such as **guidelines** (*e.g.* guidelines set out by the Prime Minister's Office in Denmark), **memoranda**, **advice** and **summary of post-public employment restrictions** (*e.g.* provided by the US Office of Government Ethics). These non-legal instruments can complement other instruments and help explain and prescribe proper post-public employment conduct. But, like many codes of conduct, they do not usually provide enforcement mechanisms and are, therefore, less likely on their own to curb post-public employment offences.

Box 4.5 describes Finland's guidelines on post-public employment, as an example.

Post-public employment systems may utilise more than one non-legal instrument. The Australian system for the public service, for example, uses several different, but related, instruments as outlined in Box 4.6. To explain the requirements relating to post-separation contact with government, a specific circular was issued by the APS Commission (Box 4.6).

Box 4.5. **Finland: Post-public employment guidelines**

The Office of the Government as Employer in the Ministry of Finance issued the Guidelines for the Transfer of an Official to the Service of Another Employer in November 2007. The guidelines focus primarily on movement to another employer, self-employment or outside working life of officials handling information of a particularly sensitive nature.

The guidelines describe the general context of post-public employment and highlight the relevant provisions that concern: public officials' obligations to observe secrecy and non-disclosure; violation and misuse of business secrets; breach and negligent breach of official secrecy, etc. These provisions are included in primary legislations such as:

- State Civil Servants' Act (750/1994).
- Act on the Openness of Government Activities (621/1999).
- Unfair Business Practices Act (1061/1978).
- Penal Code.

In addition, the guidelines suggest that public authorities consider the merits of individual cases when deciding whether they include a special clause in the employment contract of public officials handling information of a particularly sensitive nature. When public officials are in possession of specific information, knowledge and expertise on the interests of business or the government that is not generally available to businesses, the public authorities may draw up a contract on the terms of employment together with the public official, including a special period of non-availability after the period of notice. The contract may be drawn up during the recruitment process or together with the public official upon appointment.

The maximum period of non-availability is one year, during which time the former official may not perform work for another employer. During the agreed period of non-availability, former public officials receive the equivalent sum of their former salaries (in accordance with Section 44 of the State Civil Servants' Act).

The guidelines also provide contacts where public organisations can attain further information from the Office of the Government as Employer.

Source: Finland (2007), "Guidelines for the Transfer of an Official to the Service of Another Employer", *Government Rules and Regulations*, 16 November.

There are two major points to consider when selecting a remedy for post-public employment problems amongst available options, *e.g.* legislation, codes of conduct or other legal or non-legal instruments.

Box 4.6. **Australia: Circulars on post-separation contact with government**

The Australian Public Service (APS) Commission regularly issues circulars to support implementation of important policies. Recent circulars address post-public employment issues, namely:

- Circular No. 2007/3 on Post-Separation Employment: Policy Guidelines (*www.apsc.gov.au/circulars/circular073.htm*) provides an update on the APS-wide policy on managing possible conflict-of-interest situations and other probity issues when employees leave the APS to take up employment in fields that are aligned to their APS responsibilities.
- Circular No. 2008/4 on Requirements relating to the Lobbying Code of Conduct and Post-Separation Contact with Government (*www.apsc.gov.au/circulars/circular084.htm*) was issued following the release – by the Special Minister of State and Cabinet Secretary – of the Lobbying Code of Conduct on 13 May 2008. This circular sets out new policies for public servants in relation to post-separation employment as lobbyists and contacts with professional lobbyists. The circular describes the scope and key features of the Lobbying Code of Conduct, and in particular its application to the APS.

Circulars are distributed to heads of APS departments and agencies as well as members of the Corporate Management Forum. Circulars provide contact information for further information or sensitive queries of the APS Commission's Employment Policy Adviceline.

Source: www.apsc.gov.au.

First of all, the implications of adopting one instrument over another will depend on each country's or public organisation's historical tradition and its current legal, administrative and management framework. Selected specific instrument(s) should fit into the wider integrity framework in order to ensure its (their) coherence by mutually supporting other elements already in place for managing conflict of interest, in particular, and fostering integrity and resistance to corruption, in general. The following three examples underscore the close relationship between specific instruments on post-public employment in different country contexts:

- The **United Kingdom** has a brief Civil Service Code that says little about conflict of interest, but has developed an extensive Civil Service Management Code that has a great deal to say about post-public employment in particular. Adherence to the codes is a condition of employment for public servants.
- **France** traditionally relies on hard law and sanctions contained in legislation to set standards of integrity for the whole public sector. Given existing legislation in this area, together with longstanding post-public

employment practices involving public officials moving to the private sector – known as the *pantouflage* system – French authorities have favoured legislative solutions over codes of conduct.

- The approach in **Germany** differs from those of both France and the United Kingdom. To combat corruption, Germany has traditionally relied on legislation. In 1998, however, it adopted a detailed code of conduct that takes the form of administrative guidelines, including coverage of post-public employment, that are designed to inform employees as to what constitutes unethical conduct and how to prevent or manage it.

Second, limited evidence is available on the effectiveness of specific instruments in the post-public employment system. Therefore, careful selection of an instrument should be followed up with an assessment of its functioning and a measurement of its impact, in order to review its interaction with other components of the overall values and integrity framework.

Box 4.7 presents an initiative in the US that developed a special website to provide information on post-public employment restrictions.

Box 4.7. **United States: New York City's FAQ on post-public employment restrictions**

The Conflicts of Interest Board of the City of New York developed a special website to provide information on rules related to conflict of interest in general, and post-public employment restrictions in particular. The site includes guidance and training materials, such as case examples. The following two examples highlight post-public employment problems and point out rules, together with expected standards of behaviour.

Job seeking in general

While it is possible to seek a second job when working for the City, there are several basic restrictions. Your job search must be conducted on your own time, and you may not use your City position (or letterhead) to promote your job search.

Q. I am looking for a new job outside City service. May I send my resume to a firm that does business with my City agency?

A. Yes, unless you are personally involved with that firm in your City job. In that case you will have two choices:

- ask your supervisor to have someone else deal with the firm, or
- wait until the work with the firm is over.

Remember: You may not discuss a possible job with a firm or even send them your resume as long as you are dealing with them in your City job.

Box 4.7. **United States: New York City's FAQ on post-public employment restrictions** *(cont.)*

Post-employment restrictions

Q. I am leaving my City job to work for a private company. Are there any City ethics rules that will apply to my new job?

A. Yes. No matter what your position with the City is, there are certain rules regarding post-City employment that you must follow:

- You may not appear before your old agency on business for a period of one year.
- You may never work on a particular matter or project that you were directly involved in while employed by the City.
- You may not divulge confidential City information to benefit yourself or your new employer.

Source: www.nyc.gov/html/conflicts/downloads/pdf/postemp.pdf.

Post-public employment and the overall values and integrity framework

2. The post-public employment instrument(s) is (are) linked, where feasible, with instrument(s) dealing with conflict of interest in the public sector and with the overall values and integrity framework.

Post-public employment conflict of interest is only one of several forms of conflict of interest, and conflict of interest is in turn only one of several areas of risk to integrity in the public sector. It is not surprising, therefore, that post-public employment prohibitions and restrictions are included in various instruments dealing with conflict of interest in general or other instruments of the overall integrity framework in public organisations. In the same way that the Post-Public Employment Principles presented in Chapter 3 are closely linked to the OECD Conflict of Interest Guidelines, the post-public employment system in each public sector in general, or public organisation in particular, should be connected to existing broader policies and practices for managing conflict-of-interest situations.

On the other hand, an emerging trend is that specific instruments, such as Norway's Post-Employment Guidelines for the Public Service and the Post-Employment Guidelines for Politicians, are dedicated solely to post-public employment conflict of interest. Drafting guidelines in this way provides higher visibility to the issue and prescribes prohibitions, restrictions and sanctions geared to the particular challenges each public sector or public organisation faces. In countries such as Norway, post-public employment is treated separately from other types of conflict of interest because it has emerged more recently as a matter of public concern (which has encouraged the development of specific instruments). Moreover, as previously noted, post-public employment is in several ways a distinctive variation of conflict of interest.

A growing problem of integrity frameworks is that they are composed of a variety of instruments and mechanisms that are both scattered throughout the public sector and have been added over time to deal with specific integrity problems. Consequently, ensuring that the overall integrity framework is both comprehensive (to cover all integrity issues) and coherent poses a major challenge for policy makers and managers in public organisations.

Box 4.8 provides details on the framework of post-public employment measures in place in Australia, as an example.

Box 4.8. **Australia: A framework of post-public employment measures**

The APS Values and Code of Conduct are both enshrined in primary legislation, the Public Service Act. The APS Values statement emphasises the importance of high ethical standards. This underpins provisions in the Code of Conduct against real or apparent conflict of interest in connection with APS employment and against "improper use of: *a)* insider information; or *b)* the employee's duties, status, power or authority; in order to gain, or seek to gain, a benefit or advantage for the employee or for any other person."

These broad prescriptions are followed by a detailed elaboration of the specific problem area of "Post-separation Employment" in a document entitled APS Values and Code of Conduct in Practice.* This publication is promulgated by the Public Service Commission as a "guide, not a rulebook" to assist agency heads in managing post-public employment situations. This guide notes that the Australia Public Service has few legal provisions on post-public employment, but there are some restrictions on those who want to be re-engaged after accepting a redundancy package.

* See the Australian Public Service Commission's website: *www.apsc.gov.au/values/conductguidelines.htm.*

Countries seeking to adopt post-public employment prohibitions and restrictions should adequately integrate them into their overall conflict-of-interest system – as shown in the Canadian example in Box 4.9 – as well as in the broader integrity framework.

Box 4.9. **Canada: Including post-public employment measures in codes of conduct**

An example of how the post-public employment measures can be integrated into the wider conflict-of-interest and integrity measures is shown in Canada. In addition to the legislative framework, such as the Conflict of Interest Act, post-public employment measures are included in codes of conduct for both the whole public service and the most senior officeholders:

- The Public Service Values and Ethics Code has a dedicated chapter on post-public employment. Chapter 3 on Post-employment Measures[1] establishes rules of conduct related to post-public employment. These measures complement the core public service values outlined in Chapter 1 and the general conflict-of-interest measures contained in Chapter 2 of the Code.
- The Conflict of Interest and Post-employment Code for Public Office Holders – reissued by the Prime Minister in 2006 – includes a specific part on post-public employment,[2] specifying the object, compliance measures, exit arrangements and how to deal with former public officeholders.

1. See post-employment measures for the public service at *www.psagency-agencefp.gc.ca/pol/vec-cve01-eng.asp#_Toc46202811*.
2. Part III on Post-employment Compliance Measures: *www.parl.gc.ca/ciec-ccie/en/archives/ethics_commissioner/conflicts/tcp_2006.asp*.

Defining the coverage

3. The post-public employment system covers all of the entities for which post-public employment is a real or potential problem, and meets the distinctive needs of each entity.

Post-public employment restrictions can be potentially applied to all public sector officials: elected officials, notably ministers of the government and members of the legislature; appointed officials, including political appointees; and the many employees that work in ministries and departments, agencies, public enterprises, and a wide variety of other public sector organisations. Governments are understandably tempted to impose post-public employment restrictions across the entire public sector – and this is the common pattern. Once again, however, it is important to provide sufficient flexibility and to avoid imposing unnecessarily tough restrictions on the employment rights of certain officials, or groups of officials. In Canada, separate codes were developed for the public service and public officeholders while separate guidelines on post-employment were adopted for politicians and public servants in Norway (Box 4.10).

Box 4.10. **Canada and Norway: Separate codes and guidelines**

For the most senior officials in Canada, post-public employment compliance measures were re-issued in 2006 in the Conflict of Interest and Post-employment Code for Public Office Holders and then enacted in the Conflict of Interest Act of 2007. For public servants, the Values and Ethics Code for the Public Service is an employer policy managed by Canada Public Service Agency and contains the post-public employment measures for the whole public service.

In Norway, separate guidelines were developed to provide measures for politicians in particular – the Post-Employment Guidelines for Politicians – and for the public service in general – the Post-Employment Guidelines for the Public Service – that were both adopted in 2005. These measures are applicable if they are incorporated into the employment contract of the particular employee.

Source: Canadian and Norwegian responses to OECD survey.

There are ways by which more flexibility in the post-public employment system can be introduced and the negative effects of post-public employment prohibitions and restrictions can be minimised, in particular:

- Imposing different restrictions on different public sector entities, depending on the nature and extent of the threat they pose. In New Zealand, for example, conflict of interest, including post-public employment conflict of interest is defined differently for public servants, ministers, board members of Crown companies, and other board members. Each of these entities is regulated by a different instrument as well – a code of conduct, a Cabinet manual, a statute, and guidelines respectively.
- Another possible approach is to have, for each entity, a gradation of post-public employment constraints depending on the official's level and position in the organisation. In the United States, for example, the post-public employment restrictions vary depending on the level of the official; the more senior the official is, the stricter the restraints are. However, the restraints on the matter of "negotiating for employment" are the same for all executive branch officers and employees, regardless of the level of their position (although the more senior the official, the broader the practical effect of the restraint).

The revolving door also raises concerns in international organisations, in particular the use of confidential information after leaving multilateral development banks. Box 4.11 highlights rules for senior officials and staff members in international financial institutions and the post-employment provisions of the code of conduct for commissioners at the supranational level in Europe.

Box 4.11. International Monetary Fund, World Bank Group and European Commission: Post-employment rules

The **International Monetary Fund** (IMF) includes post-public employment provisions in its Code of Conduct for Staff.[1] IMF employees are expected to observe rules on confidential information, in particular, after leaving the IMF. Former employees should not:

- Use or disclose confidential information known to them by reason of their service with the IMF.
- Contact former colleagues to obtain confidential information. IMF employees are also prohibited from providing confidential information to former colleagues, who should be treated like any other outside party.

The IMF also includes post-public employment provisions for executive directors in the Code of Conduct for the members of the Executive Board.[2] The Code, similarly to employees, requires executive directors who leave IMF not to use or disclose confidential information known to them by reason of their service with the IMF. Former executive directors should neither contact executive directors or other IMF officials – other than through official channels – to obtain confidential information. In addition, the Code requires executive directors when they negotiate for, or enter into an arrangement concerning a post-Fund employment, that such circumstances should not affect the performance of their duties. Where involvement in an IMF matter could be, or could be perceived as, benefitting the prospective employer – regardless of whether there is detriment to the IMF or their constituents – executive directors should recuse themselves.

The **World Bank Group** (WBG) set limitations on the type of work a former staff member can perform upon leaving or retiring from the WBG. After separation from the WBG, former staff members may not use public information gained while employees of the WBG for personal gain. Moreover, within two years of separation from the WBG, a staff member is not allowed to:

- perform services for any entity related to an activity in which the World Bank Group has an interest;
- participate in any project in which the former employee participated personally or substantially during employment with the WBG.

Furthermore, former WBG employees cannot apply for vendor status for a period of one year after the end of their WBG employment to allow for a cooling-off period. The WBG introduced specific provisions to prohibit consultants of the WBG to participate in project implementation for which the consultant was substantially involved in the design phase.

Box 4.11. **International Monetary Fund, World Bank Group and European Commission: Post-employment rules** *(cont.)*

The Code of Conduct for Board Officials[3] requires that, concerning arrangements for prospective employment outside the WBG, board officials not allow any circumstances to influence the performance of their duties, for themselves or for their immediate family members. Board officials are requested to disclose such negotiations or arrangements to the Ethics Committee, and also recuse themselves from involvement in or influence on matters related to that prospective employer. Moreover, within a period of one year after leaving the Board, former board officials should recuse themselves from matters related to WB dealings with their future employers. In addition, executive directors and alternate executive directors are prohibited to seek, apply for, or take up appointment to the staff of the WBG including consultant appointments and any other remunerated assignments while they serve as executive directors and alternate executive directors as well as within one year period following the end of their service.

For the **European Commission**, at its first meeting the Barroso Commission adopted the Code of Conduct for Commissioners on 24 November 2004. The Code addresses risks of a conflict of interests, including after leaving office, in order to maintain independence of commissioners.[4] The Code states that the general interest requires that in their official and private lives commissioners should behave in a manner to keep dignity of their office. In particular, when commissioners intend to engage in an occupation during the year after they left their office, whether this is at the end of their term or upon resignation, they should inform the European Commission that examines the nature of the planned occupation in a timely manner. If it is related to the content of the portfolio of the commissioner during his or her full term of office, the Commission will seek the opinion of an *ad hoc* ethics committee. The Commission will decide in the case in light of the committee's findings to determine whether the planned occupation is compatible with the last paragraph of Article 213(2) of the Treaty.

1. Point 34 of IMF Code of Conduct for Staff, July 1998, *http://imf.org/external/hrd/code.htm*.
2. Section on Post-fund Employment in the Code of Conduct for the members of the Executive Board of the IMF, revised in December 2003, *http://imf.org/external/hrd/edscode.htm*.
3. See the Code of Conduct for Board Officials, WB (effective since November 2007), 9. Outside Activities and Other Employment, Section B: Conflict of Interest at *http://siteresources.worldbank.org/BODINT/Resources/CodeofConductforBoardOfficialsDisclosure.pdf*.
4. See the Code of Conduct for Commissioners, SEC(2004) 1487/2, Section 1 on Independence and Dignity: Ethical issues at *http://ec.europa.eu/commission_barroso/code_of_conduct/code_conduct_en.pdf*.

Source: Code of Conduct for Staff, Code of Conduct for the members of the Executive Board, IMF; Code of Conduct for Board Officials, WB; Code of Conduct for Commissioners, European Commission.

Focus on risk areas

4. The post-public employment system covers all of the important risk areas for post-public employment conflict of interest.

As discussed earlier, post-public employment conflict of interest is itself a risk area of increasing importance within the broad field of conflict of interest. All types of conflict of interest pose their own risks and must be managed accordingly. The specific field of post-public employment conflict of interest has two major risk areas, namely:

a) Post-public employment conflict-of-interest situations related to interactions between the public and private sectors. Policy makers and managers may first ask whether the existing post-public employment system is sufficiently tailored to adequately address those government activities involving relations with the private sector. Only a minority of OECD countries have developed specific post-public employment measures for such risk areas as procurement and contract management, regulators, customs and tax administration, inspection, police, etc. (Box 4.12).

b) Top level public officials, including decision makers such as ministers and members of legislation, as well as political advisors, senior public servants, and chief executives and managers of state owned enterprises are the primary subject of post-public employment prohibitions and restrictions (Figure 4.2).

Interaction between the public and private sectors is a pervasive feature of government, but some aspects of this relationship are particularly problematic. For instance, public officials performing regulatory functions

Figure 4.2. **Officials with specific post-public employment prohibitions and restrictions**

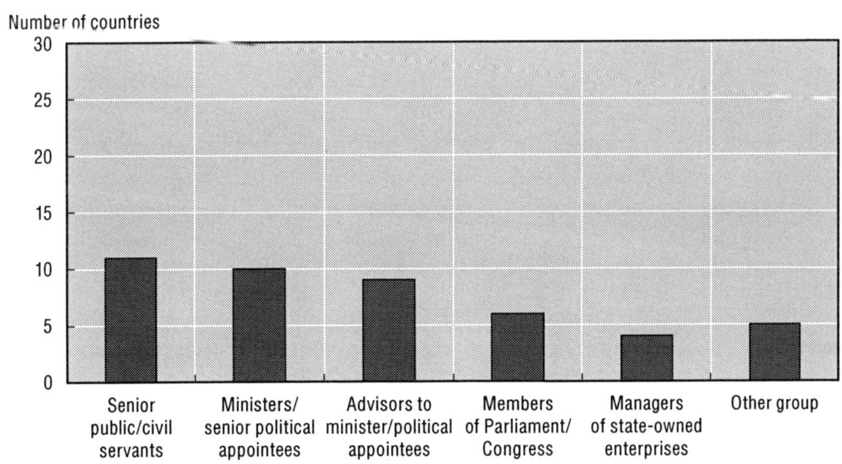

Source: OECD (2006).

Box 4.12. **Spain and Italy: Specific post-public employment restrictions**

Specific prohibitions and restrictions focus primarily on decision makers in the executive branch, in particular members of government. For example:

- The Spanish Code of Good Government and the Act on Conflicts of Interest cover high-ranking officials, including members of government and state secretaries. Similar rules are used at the sub-national level by autonomous communities.
- Italy has introduced specific prohibitions for "holders of government office", including members of government, deputy ministers, under-secretaries and extraordinary government commissioners.
- Moreover, in Italy specific prohibitions also cover at-risk areas – such as regulators in the telecom and energy sectors – as well as apply to members of the National Centre for Government Information Technology. Furthermore, specific restrictions focus on procurement and contract management for officials overseeing public works.

Source: Italian and Spanish responses to OECD survey.

have relatively more post-public employment opportunities than most other officials. And, within the regulatory sphere, such risk areas as the gaming and liqueur industries require special attention. Similarly, officials involved in customs administration, tax administration or in procurement and contract management in public private partnerships (PPP) or sponsorships are well placed to take advantage of post-public employment opportunities.

Governments may need to supplement instruments providing broad post-public employment coverage with instruments designed to minimise or manage certain risks to ensure adequate safeguards against post-public employment offences in risk areas related to interactions between the public and private sectors. An example of this approach is Australia's Strategies to Deal with Conflict of Interest in Market Testing and Outsourcing (Box 4.13).

In addition, the APS Human Resource Management Guide for Market Testing and Contracting Out[2] includes specific sections on "ethical management of the process" and "restrictions on key decision makers" that require the inclusion of a contractual provision in the requests for tender and in the services agreements that restricts the subsequent employment, or engagement as a contractor, of key decision makers in the outsourcing process for a certain period.

Another example comes from the United States where generally applicable post-public employment restrictions for federal employees are supplemented by specific provisions for those involved in procurement and contract administration, as well as in financial institution regulatory agencies (Box 4.14).

Box 4.13. **Australia: Strategies to deal with post-public employment conflict in market testing and outsourcing**

The APS Commission recognised that employees managing outsourcing or undertaking market testing are at greater risk of conflict of interest. Consequently, the Commission provides updated policy guidelines that require APS agencies to develop specific guidelines to assist employees working in these areas.

The following examples provide an indicative list of post-public employment issues and measures relevant to outsourcing and market testing:

- While it is not inappropriate for an employee to approach a successful tenderer about future employment, they must ensure they do not disclose commercially sensitive information. Information provided to a tenderer should be limited to the employee's skills, competencies, training and personal attributes. Current working arrangements should not be discussed.
- For probity, it is best that employees who occupy positions that will be outsourced be excluded from the decision-making process. Employees involved in the decision-making process should not seek to negotiate employment until the decision-making process is finalised.
- An employee managing outsourcing or undertaking market testing who is offered employment should inform their agency in writing.
- An employee should not solicit the employment of other employees on behalf of a tenderer or contractor.
- Employees must not solicit gifts, favours, or other benefits from tenderers or contractors.
- An employee should not favour former APS employees who work for tenderers or contractors.

Source: APS Circular No. 2007/3 on Post-Separation Employment: Policy Guidelines, *www.apsc.gov.au/circulars/circular073.htm*.

Another risk area, as noted before, concerns politicians and public servants working at senior levels of government and public service. In general, these officials enjoy comparatively attractive post-public employment opportunities because of the power they exercise, the information and experience they possess, and the public funds they allocate. Post-public employment offences by senior officials tend to receive considerable public attention and media publicity, thereby reducing public confidence in the integrity of government. Post-public employment breaches by senior officials can also undermine respect for ethical behaviour in the organisation as a whole (OECD, 2009).

Box 4.14. United States: Specific post-public employment prohibitions for procurement, contract management and financial regulators

In addition to the generally applicable post-public employment restrictions for federal employees in the executive branch, certain post-public employment prohibitions are applied for specific groups of employees involved in procurement functions and contract administration, and for certain officials in financial institution regulatory agencies.

Procurement and contract administration – former officials may not accept compensation from a contractor for one year as an employee, officer, director or consultant of the contractor if they:

- served, at the time a contract exceeding USD 10 million was awarded, as a procuring contracting official, or a source selection authority, or a member of the source selection evaluation board, or chief of a financial or technical evaluation team; or
- served, for a contract exceeding USD 10 million, as an administrative contracting officer, or programme manager or deputy programme manager; or
- personally made a decision to award a contract, subcontract, task order or delivery order over USD 10 million; established overhead or other rates in excess of USD 10 million; approved issuance of contract payment(s) in excess of USD 10 million; or paid or settled a claim for more than USD 10 million.

Financial institution regulatory agencies – officers and employees of federal banking agencies, a Federal Reserve Bank or the National Credit Union Administration who have, for at least 2 months of the last 12 months of employment, served as the senior examiner with continuing broad responsibility for the examination of a specific depository institution or depository institution holding company ("examined entity"), are prohibited for one year following termination of employment with the regulatory body from accepting compensation as an employee, officer, director or consultant from the examined entity, or any other holding company or other company that controls or is controlled by the examined entity.

Source: US response to OECD survey.

While OECD countries in general tend to focus on post-public employment prohibitions and restrictions at senior levels of government, much less attention is paid to officials lower down the totem pole, including those in specific at-risk areas, such as regulators and procurement officials. Even lower-level officials such as secretaries and clerks have access to confidential information that they could exploit for private gain. This strengthens the argument to cover employees below the most senior levels of various public sector organisations, though differing degrees of restraint should be tailored to the risk of conflict of interest in their post-employment.

OECD countries are increasingly establishing and strengthening specific restrictions on lobbying back to government, for example in Australia (Box 4.15), Canada and the United States (Box 4.16), as well as France, Korea, Mexico, Netherlands, Portugal, Turkey and the United Kingdom.

Countries are also growing increasingly concerned about the private use of results of scientific research (*e.g.* resulting in a pattern) that may also raise copyright issues. Countries are also concerned about memoirs published by former senior officials (Box 4.17).

Box 4.15. **Australia: Lobbying Code of Conduct establishes prohibitions on post-public employment lobbying**

The Australian Lobbying Code of Conduct was released in May 2008 to establish prohibitions on engaging in lobbying activities by former officials in the public service, namely:

- In the public service senior executives and equivalents have a one-year cooling-off period in which they are prohibited from engaging in lobbying government representatives on any matters on which they have had official dealings as public servants over their last 12 months of employment. Similar rules apply to members of the defence force at the level of colonel and above.

The Code also places post-separation employment restrictions on other categories of government representatives, including:

- Former ministers and parliamentary secretaries must not engage in lobbying activities for an 18-month period after they leave on any matters on which they have had official dealings over the last 18 months in office.
- Former ministerial staff employed in the offices of ministers and parliamentary secretaries at the advisor level and above must not engage in lobbying activities for a one-year period after they leave on any matters on which they have had official dealings over their last year in employment.

Source: Lobbying Code of Conduct, Australia, 2008.

Box 4.16. **Canada and the United States: Strengthening post-public employment restrictions for senior government officials and legislators**

Although restrictions related to post-public employment lobbying had been established for many years in North America, higher expectations of transparency and integrity brought this issue back to the political agenda. Recent legislation further strengthened existing provisions on post-public employment lobbying in order to close the revolving door, respectively, in the executive and legislative branches:

- In Canada, the Prime Minister issued in February 2006 the Conflict of Interest and Post-employment Code for Public Office Holders which toughened the prohibition of post-public employment lobbying for certain public office holders for a period of five years after leaving public office. The Federal Accountability Act (FAA), one of the government's top five priorities on taking office in February 2006, made substantive changes to 45 statutes, including the Lobbyist Registration Act. In the implementation of the FAA, several new legislations addressed post-public employment issues, including the new Conflict of Interest Act and the new Lobbying Act. The latter, which came into force in July 2008, extends the five-year ban on lobbying to a broader group of individuals named "former designated public office holders" (DPOHs). This category includes both politicians such as ministers, minister of state, ministerial staffers and former designated members of the Prime Minister's transition team as well as senior executive positions in the public service, for example deputy minister or chief executive officer.
- In the United States, the Honest Leadership and Open Government Act (HLOGA) was enacted in September 2007. HLOGA includes amendments to the post-public employment restrictions by extending the one-year cooling-off bar for Senators and Cabinet level officials to two years and requires the House and the Senate to post on the Internet the beginning and ending dates of the restrictions for each departing legislator and staff member covered by the restriction.

Source: Lobbying Act, Conflict of Interest Act, Canada; Office of Government Ethics, United States.

Box 4.17. **United Kingdom: Publishing memoirs and commentary by former senior officials**

A series of publications of memoirs by former senior officials, including ministers and their special advisers, as well as diplomats, resulted in two inquiries in 2006 and 2007-08 by the Public Administration Select Committee (PASC) of the House of Commons in the United Kingdom. The second inquiry reviewed the shift from a former liberal regime to a more restrictive one by focusing on the following two questions:

- whether it is right that the Government should have the final say on what information can be included in memoirs;
- whether revisions made by the Foreign Office to its rules have unduly limited former diplomats' ability to contribute to public debate.

Box 4.17. **United Kingdom: Publishing memoirs and commentary by former senior officials** *(cont.)*

The PASC's 14th Report of the Session 2007-08 on *Mandarins Unpeeled: Memoirs and Commentary by Former Ministers and Civil Servants* states the following conclusions and recommendations:

1. Where there is a dispute between an author of memoirs and the Government, it does not seem right that the Government should be the arbiter of that dispute as well as a party to it (Paragraph 6).
2. We do not accept that the government of the day is best placed to judge whether it is in the public interest for particular information to be published. This does not seem consistent with the principle of freedom of information. We are disappointed, therefore, that the Government did not concede the logic of some form of appeal of its decisions, along the lines of an Advisory Committee for Memoirs. The application of our suggestions on confidentiality clauses and copyright without a commensurate appeals process shifts too much power from putative memoirists to Government (Paragraph 10).
3. The approach taken to judging public interest in publication of memoirs should be consistent with the approach taken to judging public interest in disclosure of information under the Freedom of Information Act. By passing that Act, the Government has accepted the principle that it cannot be the Government which is the ultimate arbiter of whether it is in the public interest for a particular piece of information to be published. It is indefensible to deny that principle in the specific circumstances of political memoirs. Indeed, we are not sure that the courts would uphold any bid by the Government to pursue remedy for breach of copyright when the decision to prohibit publication of certain information had not been tested independently of government (Paragraph 12).
4. We continue to believe that a new Advisory Committee on Memoirs would make for expert and specialised arbitration of issues around the publication of public service memoirs. However, although this argument was not put to us by the Government, we can see that one argument against such an Advisory Committee would be that it would involve the creation of yet another new regulatory body, with all the expense and bureaucracy that entails. Given the rarity of disputes over the content of memoirs, it may well be disproportionate to create a new body. However, there is another possible solution readily to hand. If we accept the principle that an independent body should judge the public interest in publication of particular information in memoirs, then there is already an independent body which specialises in applying public interest tests to disclosure of information which Government does not want to reveal. That body is the Office of the Information Commissioner (Paragraph 13).

Box 4.17. **United Kingdom: Publishing memoirs and commentary by former senior officials** *(cont.)*

5. An alternative to an Advisory Committee on Memoirs is that the Information Commissioner could arbitrate where there are disputes in the negotiation of the content of memoirs. The Commissioner is experienced at balancing competing public interests in openness and necessary confidentiality. In applying the Freedom of Information Act, the Commissioner is accustomed too to the entirely appropriate bias towards publication. Although the Commissioner would not necessarily have the nuanced understanding of issues around memoirs which an Advisory Committee could provide, allocating this role to the Commissioner would be simple, consistent and cost-effective. Whatever model is preferred, we call on the Government to make one final reform to complete a fair, practical system for approving memoirs (Paragraph 14).
6. The revised version of Diplomatic Service Regulation 5 is another example of the Government replacing a regime that may be too liberal with one that may be too restrictive. It is too stringent to expect people to seek clearance for anything they say that draws on any experiences they had in their entire careers. Were the rules to be applied literally, they would (among other things) prevent any live TV or radio commentary from former diplomats for the rest of their lives. They would thus substantially diminish informed discussion of major world events. The contribution of former diplomats to our understanding of what is going on in Zimbabwe, or Kenya or Pakistan, should not be underestimated. Nor should it be curtailed (Paragraph 23).
7. We cannot judge the intent behind the new rules, but the results do indeed appear to be excessively wide-ranging and oppressive. Their only saving grace is that they seem to be unworkable. In practice, the Foreign Office continues to rely on the good sense of its former staff. It should say so. There is no sense in maintaining a rule that is both wrong in principle and manifestly unworkable in practice (Paragraph 24).
8. Both in respect of memoirs and in respect of public commentary by former diplomats, a pendulum has swung since our inquiry in 2006. Government was understandably concerned that a too liberal regime was having deleterious effects on trust and frankness between politicians and officials; but in tackling this problem, it has created new ones. In this report we have drawn out two important respects in which, having once been too liberal, the Government has now set up a regime which may instead be unduly restrictive (Paragraph 25).

Source: PASC (Public Administration Select Committee) (2008), 14th Report of the Session 2007-08 on *Mandarins Unpeeled: Memoirs and Commentary by Former Ministers and Civil Servants*, *www.publications.parliament.uk/pa/cm200708/cmselect/cmpubadm/664/664.pdf*.

The "cooling-off" period

5. *The restrictions, in particular the length of time limits imposed on the activities of former public officials, are proportionate to the gravity of the post-public employment conflict of interest threat that officials pose.*

Earlier discussion noted the desirability of time limits, or a cooling-off period, for managing the contacts of former officials with public sector organisations. Time limits are a frequent feature of efforts to deal with the problem areas of post-public employment lobbying, switching sides and using insider information. Although the overall aim of the cooling-off period is to maintain confidence in government and public decision making, it can also provide a learning period for both former officials and those in the government to become used to their new relationship *vis-à-vis* one another, and ensure that decisions are not influenced by previous relationships, be they friendship or animosity.

There is substantial variation from country to country and also within countries in the length of the time limits adopted to ward off post-public employment offences. As the following example in Mexico shows (Box 4.18), the application of conflict-of-interest legal provisions for public officials may be extended for a one-year period after leaving public service.

Although debates often focus on the length of the cooling-off period, length is less important than whether the limits are effective in preventing and managing post-public employment conflicts of interest and whether the limits are fair, proportionate and reasonable in light of the seriousness of the potential offence. In the problem areas of switching sides and using insider

Box 4.18. **Mexico: Post-public employment prohibitions**

The Federal Law on Public Officials' Administrative Responsibilities in Mexico[1] extends the application of general conflict-of-interest provisions[2] for an additional year for public officials after they leave their functions. The law also establishes the following specific prohibitions:

- "In no case will he use his influence or obtain any advantage derived from the function he performed, for himself or for his spouse or blood relatives up to the fourth degree, his in-laws, or for third parties with whom he has professional, labour or business relations, or for partners or companies that the public official or the above-mentioned persons are or have been a part of.
- He will not make advantageous use for his own or another's benefit, of the information or documentation he has had access to during his employment or commission and that is not within the public domain."

Box 4.18. **Mexico: Post-public employment prohibitions** *(cont.)*

Additional restrictions exist for specific groups leaving from other public organisations, namely:

- Public officials holding top-level management posts in the Federal Electoral Institute, its board members, and the Magistrates of the Federal Judicial System's Electoral Court should abstain from participating in any public office of the administration that is headed by whoever won the election that they organised or processed.
- Heads of internal control units in the federal agencies and entities, and in the Attorney General's Office, as well as heads of auditing and complaints must abstain from accepting employment in the public institution they supervise, evaluate, investigate and control in order to avoid incurring conflicts of interest.[3]

1. Articles 8 and 9, Paragraph XII of the Federal Law on Public Officials' Administrative Responsibilities.
2. According to the general conflict-of-interest provision, public officials shall abstain from soliciting, accepting or receiving personally or through other person, money, personal or real property *via* transfer at a price much lower than in the market, donations, services, employment, offices or commissions for themselves personally or for individuals with whom they have family, personal or business relations, that originate from any individual or legal entity whose professional, commercial or industrial activities are directly tied to, regulated or supervised by the public official involved, in the performance of employment and that implies conflict of interest.
3. This standard was issued by the Minister of Public Administration in Official Bulletin No. SP/100/0329/2003 on 30 May 2003.

Source: Federal Law on Public Officials' Administrative Responsibilities, Mexico.

information, fixing time limits in terms of months or years is usually inappropriate because the duration of the threat cannot be predicted in advance. It is linked to the life of the matter and lasts until the relevant procedure or negotiation on a contentious issue is finished. Concerning insider information, the ban remains valid until the information is unclassified or made public.

As senior officials pose a greater risk, time limits are more commonly applied, or are applied more strictly, to decision makers, politicians and senior public servants than to other officials. For example, Canada's experience with post-public employment offences has resulted in a longer disqualification period for Cabinet ministers (extended from two years to five years) than for other public officeholders and for public servants in executive positions (one year) (Box 4.19).

Time limits in general range from one year (*e.g.* in Ireland, Poland and the Slovak Republic) to two years (*e.g.* in Japan, Korea, the Netherlands, Turkey and the United Kingdom). A six-month maximum period was introduced by the Post-Employment Guidelines for Politicians in Norway.

Box 4.19. **Canada: A one-year limitation period for public servants in executive positions**

For a period of one year after leaving office, Canadian public servants in executive positions cannot:

- accept an appointment to a board of directors of, or employment with, entities with which they personally, or through their subordinates, had significant official dealings during the period of one year immediately prior to the termination of their service;
- make representation for, or on behalf of, persons to any department or organisation with which they personally, or through their subordinates, had significant official dealings during the period of one year immediately prior to the termination of their service;
- give advice to their clients using information that is not available to the public concerning the programmes or policies of the departments or organisations with which they were employed or with which they had a direct and substantial relationship.

Source: Values and Ethics Code for the Public Service, Canada. See the "Limitation Period" Section in the code, available at *www.psagency-agencefp.gc.ca/pol/vec-cve01-eng.asp#_Toc46202811*.

Time limits may be tailored to the level of public officials and specific groups or a particular risk area, as the following Canadian examples show:

- For public servants, one year is the general time limit in Canada, while for ministers a two-year period is applied.
- A specific five-year ban on lobbying was introduced recently for ministers, ministerial staffers and senior public servants.

In Germany, the five-year cooling-off period as a maximum can be applied for civil servants if they leave service before they reach retirement age, which is 65. However, this time limit is up to three years in the case of retiring civil servants and during the period when they receive a transitional allowance (usually two years but maximum three years) for fixed-term volunteer soldiers.

When public officials definitively leave public service in France, for a period of five years they cannot:

- exercise private activities determined by the administration;
- participate financially in private enterprises that have a relationship with the former public sector employer.

While in certain cases a persuasive argument can be made for time limits as long as five years, allowing some discretion in the application of the limits will help ensure fairness and avoid unduly strict constraints on the rights of former officials.

Providing flexibility in the application of general rules in individual cases is an emerging concern in countries. In Japan, the head of the employer government agency can apply for an exception to the post-public employment restrictions[3] to the National Personnel Authority, and needs its approval to make an exception to the rules. Members of government and high-ranking officials in Spain will not breach incompatibility regulations when they return to the private company in which they worked before being appointed as long as the activity they are going to carry out in the private sector is not directly related to the competencies of their previous office, or where they cannot take decisions related to that office.

Applying flexibility in concrete cases may require standards to ensure fairness in the process and accountability of decisions. However, only a few OECD countries have actually developed standards against which post-public employment approval decisions can be made. Some countries include them in legal provisions, for example in France and Mexico. In the United States, both restrictions and standards for exceptions and issuing waivers are set forth in statute.[4] Canada spells out criteria that a deputy head – the administrative head of a department – can use as a basis for waiving or reducing the limitation period for public servants in the Public Service Values and Ethics Code (Box 4.20).

Box 4.20. **Canada: Criteria for reducing public servant time limits**

In Canada, every case is reviewed on a case-by-case basis to determine if there is a real, apparent or potential conflict of interest between the new employment of former public servants and their most recent responsibilities within the federal public service. The Values and Ethics Code for the Public Service outlines the restrictions as well as six circumstances under which the one-year limitation period could be reduced or waived. The deputy head can waive or reduce the limitation period for a public servant or former public servant, taking into consideration the following factors:

- the circumstances under which the termination of their service occurred;
- the general employment prospects of the public servant or former public servant;
- the significance to the government of information possessed by the public servant or former public servant by virtue of that individual's position in the public service;
- the desirability of a rapid transfer of the public servant's or former public servant's knowledge and skills from the government to private, other governmental or non-governmental sectors;
- the degree to which the new employer might gain unfair commercial or private advantage by hiring the public servant or former public servant;
- the authority and influence possessed while in the public service, and the disposition of other cases.

Source: Values and Ethics Code for the Public Service, Canada. See the "Reduction of Limitation Period" Section in the code, available at *www.psagency-agencefp.gc.ca/pol/vec-cve01-eng.asp#_Toc46202811*.

Public officials in risk areas such as regulation or contract administration may require specific restrictions, including longer time limits as well.

Post-public employment conflict of interest situations also happen in public organisations at the sub-national level. Consequently, various governments set restrictions and a "cooling-off" period for their former officials at state, regional and municipal levels. The following Box 4.21 highlights the limitations on former state officials' actions and the "cooling-off" period applied in Wisconsin, US.

Box 4.21. **Wisconsin, US: Post-employment limitations on former state officials' actions**

Wisconsin's law prohibits former state officials from benefiting from their former governmental positions to advance their private interests. They include the following restrictions:

- *Appearance before former agency* – For 12 months after leaving office, a former state official should not, as a paid representative of anyone other than a governmental entity, either appear before or try to settle or arrange a matter by calling, writing, or conferring with an officer or employee of the agency with which they were associated during the last 12 months of their service as state official.
- *Appearance before other agencies* – 12-month waiting period on matters for which formerly responsible. For 12 months after leaving office former state officials should, as a paid representative of anyone other than a governmental entity, neither appear before nor negotiate with a state officer or employee about a judicial or quasi-judicial proceeding of the kind for which the former official was responsible during the last 12 months of their service as a state official or about an application, contract, claim, or charge that might lead to such a proceeding.
- *Matter in which personally and substantially involved* – A former state official may never act as a paid representative of anyone other than the State of Wisconsin in a judicial or quasi-judicial proceeding or an application, contract, claim, or charge which might give rise to such a proceeding if the former official participated personally and substantially in the matter as a state official.

These limitations apply to former state officials, whether paid or unpaid, other than officers, members, and employees of the legislature and its service agencies.

Source: Section 19.45(8), Wisconsin Statutes, Wisconsin Ethics Board, *http://ethics.state.wi.us.*

Communicating post-public employment rules

6. The restrictions and prohibitions contained in the post-public employment system are effectively communicated to all affected parties.

Successful implementation significantly depends on vigorous dissemination to reach out to all relevant parties with a role in the post-public employment system, including in the public, private and non-profit sectors. There is no single "magic bullet" to ensure that public officials and prospective employers understand and follow post-public employment rules. Thus, a variety of means in line with relevant components of the Integrity Framework should be considered to communicate post-public employment rules. The Civil Service Management Code in the United Kingdom, for example, contains several procedures for "making staff aware of the [post-employment] rules". In the United States, this responsibility is left to individual federal agencies.

The most common communication measures in OECD countries include briefings, counselling and advice. These might include formally briefing new employees on post-public employment requirements and formally reminding departing employees of post-public employment restrictions in exit interviews or by letter. Current public officials also need to be sensitive to the post-public employment rules, in part because:

- Post-public employment offences can begin before officials actually leave the public sector, for example in the form of negotiation of future employment.
- Current public officials are responsible for preventing conflict of interest when dealing with former officials (*e.g.* not granting preferential treatment, special access or privileged information to former officials).

Briefing on appointment and before leaving public office is the most frequently used measure in OECD countries. All new staff receives the Civil Service Code of Standards and Behaviour at a briefing session on appointment in Ireland. In the Canadian Public Service, a copy of the Values and Ethics Code for the Public Service is attached to the letter of offer for all new and subsequent appointments. In Spain, the Directorate General of Public Administration sends a reminder to high-level officials when they join or leave public office.

Counselling public officials about post-public employment requirements can be *ad hoc* – when officials require – or on a regular basis, in the form of an annual formal letter or as part of integrity training programmes designed to bolster officials' knowledge of the overall values and integrity framework. Like leadership by example, integrity training can substantially influence the ethical climate of organisations and conduct of public officials. Comprehensive integrity training integrates post-public employment issues as an essential part of the programme and gives proper consideration to special training measures for employees working in at-risk areas. In the United States, for example, in addition to educational or training materials prepared by individual federal agencies, the Office of Government Ethics (OGE) posts on its website an annual list of conflict-of-interest prosecutions and a digest of its informal opinions, both of which may have information dealing with post-public employment (Box 4.22).

Box 4.22. **United States: Communicating measures to implement post-public employment rules**

In the United States, advice given may be kept in written form, depending upon the agency's practice, or at the request of the individual requestor. Depending upon practice, the agency may issue general educational or training materials using sanitised versions of real situations. Current employees who are aware of the post-public employment restrictions may also be sensitive to any contacts they may have with a former official and may seek advice with regard to those contacts, particularly if they believe the contacts may violate the post-employment statute. A public official sensitive to post-public employment restrictions can both avoid misconduct when leaving government service as well as identify potential misconduct of others.

Each year, the Office of Government Ethics compiles a description of all of the prosecutions of the criminal conflict-of-interest statutes, including 18 USC 207 and makes that description available on its website.* The compilation includes the name of the individual convicted, a short description of the conduct, and any sentence imposed.

Specific prospective employers may request information from the ethics official on the application of the statutes, and general information is provided to the private sector through various training/seminar venues that focus on government ethics and the private sector. Additionally, OGE maintains a digest of its informal opinions on the OGE website (*www.usoge.gov/pages/advisory_opinions/advisory_opins.html*), many of which address post-employment restrictions.

* The Conflict of Interest Prosecution Surveys from 1990 to 2004 can be consulted at *www.usoge.gov/pages/laws_regs_fedreg_stats/other_ethics_guidance.html*.

Another mechanism for communicating post-public employment rules is the inclusion of reference to the rules in contractual and other arrangements between public sector and private sector organisations. As mentioned above, the strategies and measures used by the Australian Public Service – in particular in the tendering, contracting and market testing procedures – are noteworthy (Box 4.23). The principal source of guidance for agencies about post-separation employment in particular, and conduct issues in general, is the APS Values and Code of Conduct in Practice.[5]

Box 4.23. Australia: Communicating post-public employment rules to the private sector

Australia targets the private sector as well when it communicates post-public employment rules and expected conduct. As a result, 77% of Australian Public Service agencies reported defining and communicating agency's expectations to non-public servants to comply with the relevant APS Values and Code of Conduct. Of these:

- 75% did so through information set out in tender documentation.
- 78% reported using general clauses in contracts referring to the APS Values and Code of Conduct.
- 25% reported including specific contractual clauses regarding only relevant aspects of the Values and Code of Conduct.
- 22% of relevant agencies reported using non-contractual arrangements such as briefing sessions, protocols and integrity training.

Source: APS (2004), "State of the Service Report 2003-2004".

The rules can also be communicated through a government structure, in which integrity actors, such as the Office of the Conflict of Interest and Ethics Commissioner in Canada, play a central role in providing advice on post-public employment obligations to former public officeholders. In the United States the Office of Government Ethics provides branch-wide regulations and policy guidance. Agency ethics officials typically provide the actual advice to departing officials using that guidance. In Ireland, former officers below the assistant/secretary level must apply to the secretary general or head of office in which they last served before retirement or resignation, whereas officers at and above the assistant/secretary level must apply to the Outside Appointments Board.

Authorities and arrangements

7. The authorities, procedures and criteria for making approval decisions in individual post-public employment cases, as well as for appeals against these decisions, are transparent and effective.

Although the vast majority of OECD countries set general rules for preventing conflict of interest in post-public employment, a minority of them have established mechanisms to apply these rules in practice. While these countries employ measures for communication, such as briefings on appointment and on departure discussed in the previous section, only a few countries have developed clear and effective measures to apply the prohibitions and restrictions adopted. In Canada, Ireland, Portugal and Spain, for example, it is required that officials disclose future employment plans and obtain approval

Box 4.24. United States: Procedures for providing information on future employment

Although there is no legal requirement for executive branch officials to report their seeking or negotiations for a non-government position, the criminal provisions on negotiating future employment require the individual to recuse from matters that have a direct and predictable effect on the financial interests of the prospective employer. Recusal often necessitates an explanation so that others understand why the individual cannot continue to work on particular matters.

Those individuals who are required to file "public financial disclosures" must report any arrangements with future employers on their financial disclosure forms. These arrangements must be disclosed in the disclosure form to the extent an arrangement exists at the time the report is required to be filed.

Source: US response to OECD survey.

before taking up a new appointment. In the United States, criminal provisions require an individual to disqualify himself from matters that have a direct and predictable effect on the financial interests of the prospective employer (Box 4.24).

Determining the "integrity actor",[6] a specific authority or authorities to be responsible for implementing a post-public employment system at the national level is a complex matter that requires appropriate examination of factors such as the main implementation instrument(s) and mechanisms, the public sector entities and the risk areas covered. The influence of each government's institutions, structures, processes and culture within which the authorities for handling post-public employment matters must be set is also critically important.

Managers play a key role as integrity actors in post-public employment systems in particular, and in building a sound integrity framework in general. For example, agency heads in the Australian Public Service are responsible for ensuring that measures to manage conflicts of interest, including post-employment cases, are applied effectively in their agencies. This also requires that employees need to be made aware of their responsibilities to disclose and take reasonable steps to avoid conflicts of interest, and that procedures are in place to deal with situations where it appears that individuals have not met their responsibilities.

OECD countries are increasingly establishing separate government-wide integrity agencies as integrity actors to administer and enforce integrity standards, including post-public employment prohibitions and restrictions. The establishment of an Ethics Commission in France (Box 4.25) is an example of this.

Box 4.25. France: Ethics Commission handles individual post-public employment cases

The movement of public servants to the private sector – the so-called *pantouflage* – is a highly regulated practice in the French public service as it is subject to judiciary, regulatory and legislative checks and controls. Following the Law on the Prevention of Corruption, approved in January 1993, three ethics commissions – *Commissions de déontologie* – have been set up, one for each segment of the public service: *i)* the central government service; *ii)* the territorial authorities; *iii)* the public hospital sector.

It became obligatory for officials to consult these commissions before moving to the private sector for any reason. After almost 15 years' experience, based on the Public Service Modernisation Law of February 2007, the Decree of 1 June 2007 created a single Ethics Commission with the aim of centralising these three committees and reinforcing transparency. The Ethics Commission* – *Commission de déontologie de la fonction publique* – handles all individual cases related to post-public employment and the accumulation of activities.

The Commission is headed by a member of the Council of State and is composed of members from the Court of Auditors, from the courts as well as from the Inspector General's Office and specialised public servants. The Commission reports to the Prime Minister, which indicates its importance to the government.

* *www.fonction-publique.gouv.fr/rubrique97.html.*

Source: OECD (2004), *Managing Conflict of Interest in the Public Service: OECD Guidelines and Country Experiences*, OECD, Paris.

Some countries have dedicated more than one integrity office to dealing with different government entities and public sector organisations. Canada, for example, established the Office of Conflict of Interest and Ethics Commissioner for public officeholders, including Cabinet ministers and the most senior levels of the public service and members of the House of Commons. Moreover, a separate Ethics Officer for the Senate is in charge of the upper house of Parliament (Box 4.26).

Although the context and pressure to identify authorities and arrangements to implement and enforce post-public employment rules may vary from one country to another, there are two general considerations to keep in mind when determining the options all jurisdictions need to take into account:

- First, clearly designate the authority or authorities responsible for administering the main implementation instrument(s). Politicians, public servants and other government entities can be subject to the same authorities or to separate ones. Moreover, a single entity such as a government

Box 4.26. **Canada, Italy and Spain: Integrity actors for post-public employment**

In Canada, the Conflict of Interest Act came into force in July 2007, which strengthened the role of the new Conflict of Interest and Ethics Commissioner. The Commissioner has judicial or quasi-judicial background with powers to fine violators of the Conflict of Interest Act and consider public complaints. In addition, a new independent Commissioner of Lobbying was established in July 2008 with a strong mandate to investigate violations under the Lobbying Act and Lobbyists' Code of Conduct.

In Italy, the 2004 Conflict of Interest Act assigns independent authorities, including the Competition Authority, to enforce the application of post-public employment rules established by the Act. In addition, the High Commissioner for preventing and combating corruption and other forms of illicit conduct can monitor and investigate offences related to post-public employment.

In Spain, the Office of Conflict of Interest is the central authority for managing the post-public employment measures of members of government and senior civil servants when they move to the private and non-profit sectors. The office, under the supervision of the Minister of Public Administration, collects relevant information to make approval decisions in accordance with the 2006 Act on Conflicts of Interest.

Source: Conflict of Interest Act, Lobbying Act, Canada.

department or other public sector organisation may have the content of its post-public employment system determined by a central government at the national level but receive delegated authority to implement the regime. This approach helps to ensure consistency in the rules and permits flexibility in their interpretation, but cannot guarantee fair and consistent rule application across the whole public sector.

- Second, authorities should clearly identify and communicate the procedures to be followed by officials contemplating leaving government and the criteria for approval decisions in individual post-public employment cases. With regard to procedures, governments can, for example, require that public officials disclose offers of future employment that involve a risk of conflict of interest and seek the employer's permission before accepting an offer.

Making approval decisions on post-public employment cases generally falls under the responsibility of the top management of public organisations: the secretary general of departments in Ireland, the head of the organisation for civil servants in Norway, the deputy head of public organisations for public servants in Canada. These deputy heads generally delegate their authority to make approval decisions on individual post-public employment cases;

however, they may not delegate their accountability for ensuring that the code is fully upheld and advanced within their organisations. In Spain, the Directorate General of Public Administration centralises the approval decisions on post-public employment of high-ranking officials. An example of centralisation is the recent establishment of the Centre for Personnel Interchanges between Government and Private Entities in Japan (Box 4.27).

Box 4.27. **Japan: Measures to improve fairness and transparency in post-retirement employment**

Up to the last amendment, the National Public Service Act had stipulated that officials shall not, for a period of two years after separation from the service, accept or assume a position with a profit-making enterprise that has a close connection to any agency of the State defined by rules of the National Personnel Authority, any specified independent administrative institution, with which such persons were formerly employed within five years prior to separation from the service. This prohibition was exempted only if *ex ante* approval of the National Personnel Authority was given to the official concerned.

However, the Act was amended in June 2007, in order to activate mobility of personnel between the national government and the private sector, as well as to realise fair and transparent employment after retirement from the public service.

The amendment stipulates that:

- In effect by the end of 2008, each ministry or other equivalent government entity shall not provide assistance to support post-retirement employment to its employees and retired employees.
- The Centre for Personnel Interchanges between Government and Private Entities, which shall be newly established under the Cabinet Office, exclusively provides such services.
- During the transition period leading up to the full functioning of the Centre, within three years beginning from enforcement of the last amendment of the National Public Service Act, each ministry and other equivalent government entity can provide post-retirement job placement services, only if the *ex ante* approval be given by the Prime Minister, the authority of which shall be delegated to the Re-employment Surveillance Commission.
- The authority to give *ex ante* approval for the post-retirement employment mentioned above, previously executed by the National Personnel Authority, shall be transferred to the Cabinet.

Source: Japanese response to OECD survey.

Within a period of one year after leaving a state managerial position in Poland, an official is obliged to obtain the consent of a special commission responsible to the Prime Minister to undertake employment in an entity previously supervised by the applicant. Recent legislation on conflict of interest refined the procedure for approval decisions in Spain (Box 4.28).

Box 4.28. **Spain: Procedure for approval decisions**

The Act, approved in May 2006, on Conflict of Interest introduced the following administrative process to prepare approval decisions related to the post-public employment conflict-of-interest cases of high-ranking officials, including ministers and secretaries of state:

- First, former high-ranking officials should inform the Office of Conflict of Interest before undertaking any future employment activity.
- The Office of Conflict of Interest will analyse the situation and consider whether or not the activity violates the law.
- The Office of Conflict of Interest will communicate its opinion to the interested party.
- The interested party is allowed to reply and provide further information for consideration.
- Finally, the Office of Conflict of Interest will make an approval decision and communicate it to the former high-ranking official.

Source: OECD (2006b), "Modernising Conflict of Interest Legislation: The Spanish Experience", OECD, GOV/PGC/ETH(2006)2.

Post-public employment guidance can include the requirement that officials making approval decisions on individual post-public employment cases should consult:

- A central government agency or a special integrity committee or advisory board: a requirement that will help to promote equitable and consistent approval decision making across public sector organisations. Central government agencies and entities involved in the consultation include the Legal Affairs Unit in the Ministry of Public Administration in Mexico and the Canada Public Service Agency for federal public servants. Independent committees also take part in consultations, for example the Ethics Commission in France, the Government Ethics Committee and the Anti-Corruption and Civil Rights Commission in Korea, and the Outside Appointments Board in Ireland.

- Entities where the public official has worked before: this requirement could substantially lead to an informed approval decision on future employment by defining the types and the extent of actual and potential conflict of interest, as the German example shows in Box 4.29.

Box 4.29. **Germany: Consultation process for approval decisions on future employment**

In Germany all relevant previous employers – those sections and departments in which the civil servant or soldier has worked during the five years prior to the end of service – are asked to verify whether it may have been possible for the civil servant or soldier to have had an influence on the economic concerns of his/her future employer or contractual partner.

The relevant sections and departments are also asked about the extent of "official knowledge" of the civil servant or soldier concerned.

Source: German response to OECD survey.

Appropriate approval decisions can also be fostered by setting clear standards, not only in regard to whether the official should be permitted to take up a particular post-public employment opportunity, but also in regard to how stringently the rules should be interpreted and exceptions granted. Such criteria can be set out in legislation, as Box 4.30 shows.

Box 4.30. **Canada: Exemptions for ministerial staff**

In Canada, the Ethics Commissioner may provide a reduction/waiver of certain restrictions – such as prohibition on contracting and on representations – for former public office holders. The Conflict of Interest Act* specifies the criteria for granting exemption to a former reporting public office holder who was a member of ministerial staff and worked on average 15 hours or more a week. Exemption may only be granted on the following criteria:

- The person was not a senior member of ministerial staff.
- The person's functions did not include the handling of files of a political or sensitive nature, such as confidential cabinet documents.
- The person had little influence, visibility or decision-making power in the office of a minister of the Crown or a minister of state.
- The person's salary level was not commensurate with the person having an important role in that office.

* See Article 38 under Rules for Former Reporting Public Office Holders at *http://ciec-ccie.gc.ca/resources/Files/English/Public%20Office%20Holders/Conflict%20of%20Interest%20Act/CONFLICT%20OF%20INTEREST%20ACT.pdf.*

Source: Conflict of Interest Act, Canada.

Procedurally, officials are expected to have the right to appeal a negative post-public employment approval decision. An effective post-public employment appeal and remedy system will also help to foster core public service values of fairness and accountability. The OECD survey shows that approval decisions on post-public employment are open to appeal in a minority of OECD member countries. Appeals can be handled by a variety of administrative and judicial bodies, such as:

- An independent court or tribunal, for example in Germany, Ireland, Italy, Japan, Portugal and Turkey. In Ireland, the Secretary Generals' approval decisions on concrete post-employment cases can be appealed to the Outside Appointments Board. In Italy, the decisions of the Competition Authority on post-public employment cases can be appealed to administrative courts, with two levels of judgement.
- An administrative body within the public service, for example in Germany, Ireland and Portugal.

In the United States, there is no specific body established to review and approve departing officials' post-public employment plans. Instead, agency ethics officials can provide advice on the application of the law; this advice is not open to any formal appeal, although in very large agencies there may be an informal appeal to a centralised ethics office regarding the advice of a regional ethics officer. An individual who objects to advice that a statute may prohibit his or her planned future conduct can seek a declaratory judgement to the contrary through the courts, or decide to engage in the conduct and defend his/her conduct during any subsequent prosecution. If convicted, the individual may appeal the conviction to the next level federal court.

Box 4.31 sets out formal and informal appeal mechanisms in Norway and Canada.

Box 4.31. Norway and Canada: Formal and informal appeal mechanisms

Although no specific formal appeal procedures exist with regard to individual post-employment approval decisions in many countries, civil servants may ask for a new decision from the head of an organisation, as in Norway. Politicians may turn to the Standing Committee on Outside Political Appointments for Politicians and can ask for a meeting to discuss the assessment of their case. Experience of the first three years indicates that this appeal has been used exceptionally.

In Canada, public servants or former public servants may apply to the deputy head – the administrative head of a department – for reconsideration of any decision regarding their compliance with post-public employment measures.

Source: Chapter 5 of this report and Canadian response to OECD survey.

Enforcing the post-public employment system

8. The enforcement sanctions for post-public employment offences are clear and proportional, and are timely, consistently and equitably applied.

Both the absence and ineffective measures for tracking and enforcing compliance signals that a post-public employment system has no "teeth" or public authorities are not serious about applying prohibitions and restrictions. A seemingly comprehensive and sophisticated post-public employment system can be rendered ineffective if it does not monitor compliance, has no appropriate sanctions or does not enforce them in a timely manner.

Implementation of approval decisions on post-public employment generally remains the responsibility of former public officials in OECD countries. However, support measures employed by public organisations to track and ensure the implementation of approval decisions are rarely used; Box 4.32 indicates how they may be improved.

Box 4.32. **Measures supporting monitoring of approval decisions**

The following list illustrates the types of measures that could support the tracking of implementation and compliance with approval decisions in individual post-public employment cases. These support measures may require, for instance:

- recording the approval decisions on individual cases for future tracking, as in Canada, France, Japan, Norway and the United Kingdom;
- making available past decisions for benchmarking, as in France and Japan;
- informing prospective employers of imposed restrictions and conditions, as in Germany and the United Kingdom;
- requesting information on the application of decisions, as in Ireland and Korea.

Source: OECD, (2006b), *OECD Guidelines for Managing Conflict of Interest in the Public Service: Progress Report on Implementation*, OECD, Paris (*www.oecd.org/gov/ethics/conflictofinterest*).

The nature of the sanctions that can be imposed is closely tied to the implementation instruments discussed earlier. In general, countries employ traditional sanctions, including penal and disciplinary measures. For example, legislation can provide criminal or civil penalties. The National Public Service Act in Japan states that a person who violates post-public employment restrictions and prohibitions shall be sentenced to a prison term of up to one year or fined up to JPY 500 000. The penal sanction may range up to one year imprisonment in Korea; and in the United States the penalties can be up to five years imprisonment and a fine of not more than USD 250 000, or a multiplier of the gain or loss, whichever is greater.

In contrast to criminal or civil penalties, a code of conduct can be expected to rely on administrative remedies in the form of disciplinary measures. These administrative measures can range from mild sanctions, such as warnings and fines, to severe penalties, such as demotion and dismissal. Permitting governments to exercise discretion in choosing from this range of sanctions helps to ensure that the penalty imposed is proportionate to the nature and magnitude of the offence. For example, in the United States, civil penalties are an option to criminal prosecution and a range of administrative sanctions can be imposed, ranging from reprimand to dismissal. For another example of a sanctions system, see Italy in Box 4.33.

Box 4.33. **Italy: Sanctions system**

The Competition Authority in Italy exercises *ex post* control of new employment after leaving public office. After the appointment has been made, the Competition Authority checks its compatibility with the law on conflict of interest. If the appointment is judged "incompatible" or non-compliant, the following sanctions can be applied:

- removal or disqualification from office or position – by the competent administration or by those responsible for supervising the entity or undertaking;
- suspension of the public or private employment relationship;
- suspension of registration in professional rolls and registers, for which a request must be addressed to the professional organisations for actions within their competence.

Source: Italian response to OECD survey.

Since the scope of traditional post-public employment rules covers officials while in office, it is easier to apply sanctions for conflict-of-interest offences that occur while officials are still working in the public sector. Penalties connected with codes of conduct are especially difficult to apply to officials who have already left government. Indeed, codes lose their influence at the point where most post-public employment offences begin to arise. Nevertheless, alternative sanctions such as the cancellation or refusal of contracts with the private sector employer of the offending former official or the reduction of the official's retirement pension should be considered for inclusion in a comprehensive post-public employment regime. In Norway, former officials breaching the post-public employment guidelines can receive a penalty for default. The following box provides examples of alternative sanctions used for former officials and their employer in Spain and Germany (Box 4.34).

Box 4.34. **Spain and Germany: Sanctions for former public officials and their private sector employers**

Spain has introduced a range of innovative sanctions applicable both to former public officials who breach post-public employment rules and the private sector company that improperly employs said former public official:

- For former public officials, a declaration of a very serious, or serious, violation of the post-public employment rules is published in the *Official Gazette of the State*, which prevents the person concerned from occupying public office for five to ten years.
- For the company, non-compliance with the law is published in the *Official Gazette of the State*. It implies "debarrement" from public contracts: an automatic exclusion of the company from tender procedures during the period of the time limit of prohibitions for the former high-level official.
- As an additional civil law sanction, former officials may also risk having their public service pension reduced.

In Germany, a civil servant's or soldier's retirement pension can be curtailed in cases of breach of post-public employment rules in the federal administration.

Source: Spanish and German responses to the OECD survey.

The seriousness of sanctions may also depend on the circumstances of how the post-public employment obligations were breached. Seniority is considered in a few OECD countries (Box 4.35).

Although management measures supporting the implementation of approval decisions are exceptionally used, they may considerably encourage compliance. The communication of approval decisions on individual post-public employment cases, for instance, could enable public scrutiny. The increased media attention on cases of former politicians and high-level officials would encourage compliance with post-public employment rules and approval decisions, as the example of Norway shows in Box 4.36.

Box 4.35. **Mexico: Considering the circumstances of post-public employment breaches**

In addition to the rank and history, including seniority of the public official who commits a breach of post-public employment conflict-of-interest rules in Mexico, the Federal Law on Public Officials' Administrative Responsibilities (Article 14) defines the following circumstances for consideration in the imposition of administrative sanctions:

- the seriousness of the responsibility incurred and the advisability of eliminating practices that in any way violate the provisions of the law, or those that are enacted based on it;
- the public official's socio-economic circumstances;
- the external conditions and means of execution;
- repeated breaching of obligations;
- the amount of the benefit, gain or damage derived from the breach of official obligations.

Source: Federal Law on Public Officials' Administrative Responsibilities, Mexico.

Box 4.36. **Norway: Encouraging public scrutiny to foster compliance**

As transparency in public life is a fundamental value in Norway and the Internet provides an efficient tool for monitoring, decisions on post-public employment cases of former politicians, including ministers, political secretaries and political advisers, are directly available on the Internet.

The Secretariat of the Standing Committee on Outside Political Appointments provided by the Ministry of Government Administration and Reform prepares the cases for decision of the committee and also makes information on individual approval decisions available on its website. Public scrutiny – facilitated by high media attention – has played an important role in encouraging compliance with the *Post-Employment Guidelines for Politicians.*

Regarding former public servants, no system exists for reporting on approval decisions and their implementation as it remains the individual responsibility of former public servants. However, the Ministry of Government Administration and Reform is considering assessing the functioning of this system after collecting more information on implementation practices.

Source: Norwegian response to the OECD survey.

Measuring effectiveness

9. The effectiveness of the policies and practices contained in each post-public employment system is assessed regularly and, where appropriate, is updated and adjusted to emerging concerns.

Almost half of OECD countries have reviewed and updated their post-public employment systems in the past decade. Many of them have even further strengthened and reinforced prohibitions and restrictions, for example by:

- setting rules in legislation for providing enforceable sanctions through the Conflict of Interest Act in Canada, Czech Republic, Italy and Spain in the past four years;
- streamlining procedures to reinforce implementation and compliance, for example via a new decree in France.[7]

These efforts to modernise post-public employment systems are particularly noticeable given that countries have been liberalising their labour markets in general.

Countries have often been confronted with the limitation of existing general laws on public and civil service or codes of conduct to impose sanctions on former public officials. The recognition of this limitation by the traditional scope of the Public Administration Act in Norway led to the inclusion of post-public employment measures in public servant and politician contracts under the guidelines approved in 2005.

Another aspect of limitation is related to the application of restrictions at the sub-national level. Rules in general focus on public officials working at the national level, although post-public employment conflict-of-interest situations could similarly endanger trust in public decision making at the sub-national level.

Countries pay more attention to setting general prohibitions and restrictions for post-public employment that are applicable across the whole public service; they pay less attention to:

- addressing risk areas with specific measures tailored to the types of vulnerabilities;
- establishing mechanisms to implement rules.

Enforcing restrictions and imposing suitable sanctions remain a challenge for many countries. For example, existing sanctions can only be applied for public officials currently in office, rendering them insufficient. In Spain, the sanctions were considered ineffective and the government developed a more severe sanction regime with the new Act on Conflict of Interest approved in spring 2006. Lack of monitoring and control mechanisms to impose sanctions on former public officials is an additional challenge.

The current state of knowledge on post-public employment conflict of interest is limited, due largely to data on instruments, procedures and structures. A few countries require reporting on implementation and functioning of post-public employment systems, for example, in the form of an annual report, as is available to the public in Canada[8] and France. Box 4.37 summarises the practice of France's Ethics Commission providing an annual report to the Prime Minister.

Box 4.37. France: Ethics Commission provides an annual report on first-year activities

The French Ethics Commission, established in June 2007,[1] provides guidance, amongst others, on post-public employment and accumulation of activities. The Ethics Commission – similarly to the previous three Ethics Commissions (for more details, see Box 4.24) – submits an annual report to the Prime Minister.

The first annual report[2] of the Ethics Commission provides an overview of the individual cases the Commission treated since its creation as well as cases handled by the previous three commissions in 2007.

According to the French Criminal Code, public officials who leave the public service permanently or temporarily may not work for an enterprise which, during the previous three years (stipulated in the April 2007 Decree as an amendment, as opposed to the five-year period that the Criminal Code required previously), they managed or supervised. Also, public servants are prohibited from exercising a private activity if, by its nature or the conditions under which it is exercised, it undermines the dignity of their former administrative duties.

Cases handled in 2007 by the Ethics Commission cover numerous employment areas such as economy, finance and industry, defence, internal and external affairs, equipment, transport, agriculture and social affairs.

An individual whose professional situation is in question, or his/her human resources manager, can submit a case to the commission for treatment. The opinions of the Ethics Commission seldom confirm incompatibility; there was only one negative opinion issued in 2007. The vast majority – 94% of the opinions – are favourable under specific conditions. It is important to note that the opinions issued by the commission are enforceable by the courts.

1. *http://admi.net/jo/20070602/BCFX0755261D.html.*
2. *www.fonction-publique.gouv.fr/IMG/rapport_deontologie_2007.pdf.*

However, there is much less information available on the performance and effectiveness of instruments, procedures and structures in achieving desired results and outcomes. The data and benchmark initiative (OECD, 2009b) offers a new approach and guidance on how to collect data in key aspects of the integrity framework. The following two boxes (Box 4.38 and Box 4.39) highlight the experiences of measurement in the United States and the United Kingdom.

Box 4.38. **United States: Measuring effectiveness of prevention and enforcement**

Employee surveys organised by the US Office of Government Ethics have indicated that providing counselling for all types of questions, including post-employment questions, is more effective than simple training and education programmes.

The oversight by the private sector of the private sector and the former government employees who have been hired – as disappointed bidders have the right to challenge government contracts and the issuance of other government benefits if they believe that a conflict of interest has occurred during the process – may serve to support effective enforcement of post-public employment provisions. In addition, government employees themselves provide effective oversight for enforcing post-employment restrictions by reporting improper contacts made by former employees to ethics officials or the Office of the Inspector General.

Source: Response of US OGE to the OECD survey.

Box 4.39. **United Kingdom: Reviewing business appointment rules**

The United Kingdom has established long-standing non-statutory rules[1] requiring most senior Crown servants – permanent secretaries and deputy secretaries – to seek permission before they take up business appointments. An independent Advisory Committee on Civil Service Appointments,[2] established by the Prime Minister in 1975, provides advice to the Prime Minister, the Foreign Secretary and ministers on the application of most senior Crown servants who wish to take up outside appointments after they leave the Crown service.

The Rules on the Acceptance of Outside Appointments by Crown Servants[3] were updated in 1996 and accompanied by the *Guidelines on the Acceptance of Appointments or Employment Outside Government by Former Ministers of the Crown.*

The Advisory Committee publishes its annual report[4] on the application of the rules and guidelines, including statistical data.

Box 4.39. **United Kingdom: Reviewing business appointment rules** *(cont.)*

The business appointment rules have been reviewed in the past four years by:

- The Committee itself: it undertook an internal review in 2003 to look at, in particular, the issues that can arise when applicants seek to take up appointments in a sector with which they or their departments have had official dealings. In light of the results of the internal review, the committee may seek more in-depth information on relevant aspects in the future.
- An independent review: in 2004 the then Prime Minister commissioned Sir Patrick Brown to "review the Business Appointment Rules to ensure that they are compatible with a public service that is keen to encourage greater interchange with the private and other sectors which is essential for effective delivery in today's public service. The review will consider the operation of the system, taking account of practice overseas. It will also consider the current machinery for dealing with applications and the necessary resources".[5]
- Public Administration Select Committee (PASC) of the House of Commons: in 2006-07 PASC undertook an inquiry into the role and independence of ethical regulation of government, including the business appointments rules and processes. The committee published the following conclusions and recommendations:

  "We agree with Sir Patrick Brown that it would be appropriate for those leaving Crown service for other employment to be reminded of their continuing duty to keep confidential material confidential. However, we do not agree that this alone would be sufficient. We believe it is appropriate for the Advisory Committee to take into account the extent to which former Crown servants have been involved in particular policy issues and, if necessary, to ask applicants to delay taking up particular appointments. It may be helpful to redraft the rules to make clear that special advisers could be caught by this consideration (Paragraph 19).

  1. We believe it is inappropriate for former Crown servants to move almost directly to positions in which they may lobby former ministers or colleagues (Paragraph 20).
  2. We acknowledge that the current case-by-case approach means that those who wish to take up appointments will not be sure that they will be approved. Nonetheless we are concerned that a single sanction to be applied against a single test would not be adequate. We think there could be cases where the criterion of 'material influence' would operate in ways which blocked appropriate appointments but did not prevent inappropriate ones. We do not believe that this will provide the public with reassurance that impropriety is prevented (Paragraph 22).
  3. An approach which is more clearly tailored to individual cases is both more likely to win the assent of those to whom it applies, and is more easily defended on the grounds of public interest (Paragraph 23).
  4. We agree that if the public service ethos is to be maintained, those coming into Crown service from backgrounds in other fields should be properly inducted, and be given a clear explanation of what conduct is considered proper (Paragraph 24).

Box 4.39. **United Kingdom: Reviewing business appointment rules** *(cont.)*

5. Although Sir Patrick Brown makes some valuable suggestions for improving the Business Appointment Rules, we consider that his single test and single sanction approach is not satisfactory. It might prevent straightforward corruption, but would not deal with more insidious uses of influence, and would not command public confidence (Paragraph 25).
6. We believe that, as ACoBA itself proposes, former ministers should be required to submit proposed appointments to the scrutiny of a Business Appointments Committee. They should accept the advice given to them (Paragraph 27).
7. We believe that, to ensure consistency, the body which considers applications to take up business appointments from Crown servants should also be responsible for advising former ministers on such appointments (Paragraph 30).
8. If the civil service increasingly recruits to senior posts from outside the civil service, it will become more important for the Civil Service Commissioners to be aware of the likely career paths of those recruits. It seems at the least odd that ministers should be formally responsible for taking decisions about what jobs are suitable for former Crown servants, when their involvement in recruitment is so carefully regulated (Paragraph 36).
9. The Advisory Committee on Business Appointments has operated effectively, and we see little benefit in changing its composition, or its way of working. However, we recommend that the government considers whether decisions about future business appointments of senior Crown servants would be better taken by the Civil Service Commission than the Prime Minister or Head of the Home Civil Service. We acknowledge there are arguments in favour of the status quo, as well as arguments for change, but we believe the proposal deserves serious consideration (Paragraph 40).
10. We believe it would be appropriate for the Chairman of the Committee on Business Appointments to be a Civil Service Commissioner, to ensure a coherent and collegiate approach to both appointment and exit from the civil service (Paragraph 41)."

1. 1937 Memorandum on the Acceptance of Business Appointments by Officers of the Crown Services.
2. For further information on the committee, see *www.acoba.gov.uk/*.
3. *www.acoba.gov.uk/~/media/assets/www.acoba.gov.uk/rules%20pdf.ashx*.
4. *www.acoba.gov.uk/publications.aspx*.
5. Terms of Reference of the Review, Business Appointment Rules, SN/PC/3745, Library of House of Commons.

Source: Sixth Report of Session 2006-07 of the House of Commons Public Administration Select Committee, United Kingdom, *http://books.google.fr/books?id=j1w9btQbXUgC&dq=Sixth+Report+of+Session+2006-07+of+the+House+of+Commons+Public+Administration+Select+Committee&printsec=frontcover&source=bl&ots=VFKixvj4mB&sig=7j_tn6gcqvF2Scg82jP2Kmg2SCU&hl=fr#PPA1,M1*. Website of the Advisory Committee on Business Appointments *www.acoba.gov.uk/*.

Notes

1. For further details on distinctions between a code of conduct and a code of ethics, see OECD (2009a).
2. See at *www.apsc.gov.au/publications02/MTACOHRguidefinal.doc.*
3. The National Public Service Act stipulates that personnel are prohibited for a period of two years after leaving service from accepting or serving in a position in a profit-making enterprise which has a close connection with the agency in which they were formerly employed within five years prior to separation from the service, and the agency which is under the restriction is defined by the rules of the National Personnel Authority.
4. 18 USC 207(j) and (k) contain the standards for exceptions to, and the standards required to issue a waiver for the restrictions found elsewhere in Section 207.
5. Chapter 12 of the APS Values and Code of Conduct in Practice: A Guide to Official Conduct for APS Employees and Agency Heads deals with post-separation employment. The guide was released in 2003 to update and replace the former Guidelines on Official Conduct of Commonwealth Public Servants issued in 1995. Chapter 14 on post-separation employment of the updated APS Values and Code of Conduct in Practice can be consulted at *www.apsc.gov.au/values/conductguidelines.htm.*
6. For a description of the role and types of integrity actors, see OECD (2009a).
7. Decree No. 2007-611 of 26 April 2007.
8. Annual reports of the Conflict of Interest and Ethics Commissioner (Annual Report in respect of the Conflict of Interest Code for Members of the House of Commons and the Annual Report in respect of the Conflict of Interest Act) can be consulted at *http://ciec-ccie.gc.ca/Default.aspx?pid=23&lang=en.*

Bibliography

Australian Government (2007), "Post-Ministerial Employment", *Standards of Ministerial Ethics*, December, p. 5, *www.pmc.gov.au/guidelines/index.cfm.*

Australian Government (2008), Lobbying Code of Conduct.

Belgian Government (2007), Code of Conduct for Federal Public Officials.

Canada (2006), Federal Accountability Act, Lobbyist Registration Act, Conflict of Interest Act.

Canadian Government (2007), *Standards of Ministerial Ethics.*

European Commission (2004), Code of Conduct for Commissioners.

Finnish Ministry of Finance (2007), *Guidelines for the Transfer of an Official to the Service of Another Employer.*

IMF (1998), Code of Conduct for Staff.

IMF (2003), Code of Conduct for the Members of the Executive Board.

Ireland (1995), Ethics in Public Office Act.

Ireland (2001), Standards in Public Office Act.

Mexico (2002), Federal Law on Public Officials' Administrative Responsibilities.

Norwegian Government (2005a), *Post-Employment Guidelines for the Public Service.*

Norwegian Government (2005b), *Post-Employment Guidelines for Politicians.*

OECD (2006a), "Avoiding Conflict of Interest in Post-public Employment: Comparative Overview of Prohibitions, Restrictions and Implementing Measures in OECD Countries", OECD, GOV/PGC/ETH(2006)3, *www.olis.oecd.org/olis/2006doc.nsf/LinkTo French/NT0000B9CE/$FILE/JT00197267.PDF.*

OECD (2006b), "Modernising Conflict of Interest Legislation: The Spanish Experience", OECD, GOV/PGC/ETH(2006)2.

OECD (2008), *The State of the Public Service*, OECD, Paris.

OECD (2009a), *Towards a Sound Integrity Framework: Instruments, Mechanisms, Actors and Conditions for Implementation*, OECD, GOV/PGC/GF(2009)1.

OECD (2009b), "Components of Integrity: Tracking Trends in Government", OECD, GOV/PGC/GF(2009)2.

OECD (2009c), *Lobbyists, Government and Public Trust: Increasing Transparency Through Legislation*, OECD, Paris.

PASC (2008), *Mandarins Unpeeled: Memoirs and Commentary by Former Ministers and Civil Servants*, House of Commons, London.

Poland (1997), Limitation on Conducting Business Activity by Persons Performing Public Functions Act.

Spain (2006), Act on Conflict of Interest replacing the 1995 Law on Incompatibilities of High-Ranking Public Officials.

Spanish Government (2004), *Code of Good Government.*

Turkey (1981), Law on Prohibitions of Post-public Employment (Law No. 2531).

WB (2007), Code of Conduct for Board Officials.

WB (2009), *A discussion of the implications for senior management when financial institutions move into the "public domain"*, OECD Global Forum, *www.oecd.publicgovernanceforum.org/downloads/documents/Public%20%20private%20sector%20ethics.pdf.*

Chapter 5

The case of Norway

This chapter highlights the concerns about post-public employment addressed by the Norwegian Parliament in the late 1990s and puts them into context. It summarises the key steps taken in the development of guidelines for the Norwegian public service and politicians, as well as their key features and mechanisms for implementation. Finally, emerging lessons learned from the application of the two guidelines are highlighted.

Annexes to Chapter 5 are available on line at the links below:

5.A1. Post-Employment Guidelines for Politicians:
http://dx.doi.org/10.1787/735516772805

5.A2. Post-Employment Guidelines for the Public Service:
http://dx.doi.org/10.1787/735536866404

5.A3. Ethical Guidelines for the Public Service:
http://dx.doi.org/10.1787/735573105756

Introduction

Concerns about impropriety in post-public employment and practice of transfers from political positions to the public service reached the agenda of the Norwegian Parliament (*Storting*) in the late 1990s. The process of developing guidelines on post-employment for the public service took several years. The *Storting* asked the government to clarify problems and ambiguity that can arise in transition periods from a political position to a position in the senior civil service, and from a position in the civil service to a position outside the government administration. A report to the *Storting* (St. meld. No. 11 2000-2001) and the following Recommendation (Inst. St. No. 175 2000-2001) outlined possible solutions to be considered.

Following the 2003 OECD Recommendation on Guidelines for Managing Conflict of Interest in the Public Service, the Norwegian government reviewed the proposed solutions and approved the following three Guidelines in 2005 to foster integrity in government:

- first, the Post-Employment Guidelines for the Public Service were issued on 4 July 2005;
- after wide consultation, the Ethical Guidelines for the Public Service were published on 7 September 2005; and
- the Post-Employment Guidelines for Politicians were approved on 29 September 2005 and came into force on 17 October 2005.

An important post-public employment issue was whether a clause of "temporary disqualification" or "abstinence from involvement in certain cases"* in connection with transition to a new post should be included in all employment contracts from the beginning of an employment relationship or only where the nature of the position so requires. Based on advice from legal expertise, the final solution was to use the clause only in certain cases or for certain positions.

When the Post-Employment Guidelines for the Public Service were almost in place, the Government decided that parallel rules should be considered for politicians. Post-Employment Guidelines for Politicians were developed and came into force on 17 October 2005. The change in government in September 2005 provided the first test for the application of the guidelines.

* For definitions and details, see Chapter 1.

The Ethical Guidelines for the Public Service were published and distributed in September 2005 after extensive consultation, including a seminar in spring of 2005 for top executives in central government. These three sets of guidelines can be found in Annexes 5.A1, 5.A2 and 5.A3.

Norwegian government administration: Forward-looking reforms and emerging challenges

Why has the Norwegian government shown such a strong commitment to addressing integrity issues in the public sector over the past few years? Even though there have been fewer cases of corruption in Norway when compared with other countries, the cases that have occurred attracted a great deal of publicity and opened up a broader discussion about the fundamental mission of government and public institutions. It has also revealed the need for more information about existing statutory and non-statutory rules, having an impact on values and ethics in the public service.

Compared with many other OECD countries, Norway has been looked upon as a rather reluctant reformer, due to the fact that the economic situation has not forced Norway to make big changes in the public sector. However, in recent years a considerable number of reforms have taken place, and are still continuing in the public sector, and the government sector was reduced from 167 000 employees in 1994 to 118 000 employees in 2004. Important reform measures include:

- Management by objectives and performance was introduced throughout the State Administration in 1990.
- Sixty units changed their form of affiliation between 1988 and 1998.
- Seventy units underwent major restructuring between 2000 and 2004.

It is an open question whether all these changes, many of them creating new forms of relationship between the public, business and non-profit sectors, have been a contributing factor to the growing interest in the integrity and conduct of public servants. Giving more managerial freedom also increases the possibility for public officials to pursue their private interests and affiliation.

The level of trust in the public sector has been traditionally high in Norway, and surveys show that citizens' trust is higher when it is based on experience of direct contact with the public service. However, recent exposures of fraud and bribery, particularly in local communities, may have affected citizens' views on corruption. A 2005 survey indicated that only 10% of respondents has confidence in the authorities' ability to deter such events in the future, while 40% expressed little confidence in authorities' ability; 50% was of the opinion that corruption had increased in the public sector in Norway.

Guidelines to address post-employment concerns

The importance of mobility between the public and the private sectors without unnecessary impediments for the public service and for politicians is underlined in the introduction to both guidelines. It is also assumed that very few situations will arise that might call for the use of such measures in connection with employees moving to a new position outside the public service. Nonetheless, it was considered particularly important to take advantage of such options in cases in which special circumstances merit their use.

In connection with public officers moving from the public to the private sector, it is important to maintain public confidence both in the state administration and in civil and public servants. Integrity and impartiality are basic prerequisites for any undertaking in the public service. The public service is required to be impartial and independent and it is equally important that citizens perceive the public service as acting fairly, objectively, impartially and in compliance with established rules.

The post-employment guidelines requiring temporary disqualification and abstinence from case involvement are supplementary to a number of rules intended to protect the integrity and impartiality of the public service, including the provisions in the Public Administration Act, such as:

- competency rules;
- rules on employees' loyalty obligations;
- the general fairness requirement in the public service (including the principle against abusing authority);
- the obligation of professional secrecy;
- the management prerogative of the employer.

However, the rules concerning competency in the Public Administration Act refer to a situation where a conflict of interest may arise in the handling of a case and when the decision is made by the public service. After an employee has moved to a new position outside the public service, any conflict-of-interest situation may arise. This situation is no longer covered by the Public Administration Act.

The duty of loyalty could also place constraints on using knowledge acquired in a former employment relationship, but it is not clear how far the scope of the duty of loyalty actually extends. The obligation of professional secrecy in Article 13 of the Public Administration Act protects personal matters and trade secrets, but information about in-house conditions in the public service is rarely considered a trade secret that is subject to the obligation of secrecy.

The Post-Employment Guidelines for the Public Service

Although state administrative agencies do not normally operate in a competitive market, they may, in the same way as an employer in the private sector, have justifiable need for post-employment clauses in employee contracts. The following box (Box 5.1) presents the circumstances that could justify restrictions.

Box 5.1. Norway: Circumstances that could justify post-employment restrictions

There are three special factors in Norway that might justify actions such as temporary disqualification and/or abstinence from involvement in certain cases from the state employer:

- The need to protect internal information: The State must seek to prevent other organisations from gaining knowledge about an administrative agency's strategies and plans (*e.g.* on the formulation of policies, rules, etc.). Such knowledge could result in illegal competitive advantages.
- The need to protect other organisations' trade secrets: The State must seek to prevent one organisation from gaining access to confidential information about other organisations, including trade secrets, etc. as such knowledge could result in illegal competitive advantages.
- The need to safeguard the general public's confidence in the public service: State administrative agencies must seek to prevent suspicions that a civil servant has taken advantage of his or her position to gain special advantages for an organisation. Such suspicions could impair the general public's confidence in the administration's integrity and impartiality.

Source: Post-Employment Guidelines for the Public Service, 2005 and Post-Employment Guidelines for Politicians, 2005.

Where the nature of the position so requires a clause on temporary disqualification and/or abstinence from involvement in certain cases in connection with transition to a new position will be included in the employment contract from the beginning of an employment relationship. Such a clause will primarily be relevant for:

- key jobs, executive positions or positions with a special responsibility and influence;
- positions in close contact with the positions mentioned above;
- positions with authority to negotiate or purchase.

The guidelines provide a national framework for post-employment restrictions. However, individual employers may issue complementary post-employment guidelines as necessary. The following box (Box 5.2) presents the new measures introduced by the two guidelines.

Box 5.2. Norway: Post-employment prohibitions

Two sets of post-employment guidelines established new measures for politicians and public servants, namely:

- "Temporary disqualification": This refers to a ban for up to six months after leaving office, on an employee being employed by, or performing services for, an organisation outside the public service that has or can have contact with the employee's sphere of responsibilities as a civil servant or politician. The same applies to organisations outside the public service that, for other reasons, have or could have special advantages due to the employee's position as a civil servant or politician.
- "Abstinence from involvement in certain cases": This refers to a ban for up to one year after leaving office, for an employee to become involved in cases or areas that involve the employee's spheres of responsibilities as a civil servant or politician.

Source: Post-Employment Guidelines for the Public Service, 2005 and Post-Employment Guidelines for Politicians, 2005.

The clause in the contract requires the employee to inform the employer of any offer of new positions that he or she might consider. The employer may grant full or partial exemption from temporary disqualification and/or abstinence from involvement in certain cases based on an application from the employee.

The employee has the right to remuneration during the period of temporary disqualification. The remuneration shall correspond to the salary on leaving the position plus holiday pay.

An employment contract also covers agreed damages if the employee behaves at variance with the temporary disqualification or abstinence from involvement in certain cases, or breaches the obligation for mandatory reporting.

The Post-Employment Guidelines for Politicians

The Post-Employment Guidelines for Politicians are almost identical to the guidelines for the public service with some exceptions, primarily regarding the process and decision making on post-employment prohibitions.

The Standing Committee on Outside Political Appointments has the authority to decide that a politician should not work or provide services for an organisation outside the public service after his engagement as a minister, political secretary or political adviser. To ensure the independence of its decision making, the members of the committee are appointed by a royal decree, and they cannot be given instructions by the government.

The Standing Committee on Outside Political Appointments can rule on the following measures:

- Temporary disqualification – up to six months – will only be requested in certain cases and when there is a clear connection between the politician's previous spheres of responsibilities or duties and the relevant organisations' interest. The Standing Committee on Outside Political Appointments can also determine that a politician cannot work or provide services for an organisation outside the Norwegian public service for up to six months after leaving if special circumstances exist in connection with the person's earlier duties and responsibilities that have given or could give the organisation special advantages, or that might undermine confidence in the public service in general.
- Instead of being subject to temporary disqualification, a politician can be ordered to abstain from involvement in certain cases for up to one year, provided this adequately safeguards the interest that must be protected. The term "abstinence from involvement in certain cases" refers here to a ban on the politician becoming involved in a case or in an area where he or she has been directly involved by virtue of being a politician.

At least two weeks before starting the new position, the politician is required to voluntarily inform the committee on:

- starting a new job or accepting a position outside the public service; or
- starting a business.

This requirement does not apply if it is obvious that temporary disqualification or abstinence from involvement would not be a viable option. The obligation to provide information applies to all new positions taken up within one year of leaving public office.

Where temporary disqualifications are ordered, the politician – similarly to public servants – shall receive remuneration during the temporary disqualification period corresponding to the net salary he or she received on leaving, plus holiday pay and pension costs.

If the obligation for providing information is breached or the politician has behaved at variance with an imposed disqualification or abstinence from involvement in certain cases, the Standing Committee on Outside Political Appointments can require agreed damages to be paid to the State.

Standing Committee on Outside Political Appointments: Administrative procedures and experience of their application

When the new Government came into office on 17 October 2005, approximately 70 politicians from the former government left their offices, namely:

- the Prime Minister;
- 18 ministers;
- 34 state secretaries;
- 21 political advisers.

As of October 2008, 76 politicians raised formal cases for the Standing Committee on Outside Political Appointments. These figures also include politicians from the government that came into power on 17 October 2005. Six of the politicians were former ministers. In addition to the formal cases, the Secretariat of the Committee has also provided advice on the rules and procedures concerning the Post-Employment Guidelines for Politicians to other politicians.

Most of the politicians have raised one case, but two of them have raised six and seven cases, mostly related to their membership in boards. In two cases, the politicians have made a statement and asked the Committee to look at their case once more, referring to Article 7.2 of the Guidelines.

In the first year of application, 13 politicians, including 4 ministers, were temporarily disqualified – ranging from 3 to 6 months – and/or asked to abstain from involvement – up to 12 months – in certain cases.

All formal correspondence between politicians and the committee is open to the public, and copies of letters from the committee to the politicians are published on the Internet.

Experience so far shows that the new guidelines are taken seriously. There have been discussions in the media about some of the cases, both before and after the Committee has made its decisions. In 2007, the Committee was scheduled to submit its first report to the Ministry of Government Administration and Reform about its activities in 2005 and 2006, and also provide comments on their experience with the Post-Employment Guidelines for Politicians.

It could be said that beyond the successful application of the guidelines in individual cases it is more important that a high degree of transparency be ensured in the handling of these cases. An ongoing public debate about these issues is one of the most important measures to draw out how the implementation of the whole system is perceived.

The Ethical Guidelines for the Public Sector

Aims of guidelines

High ethical standards for the provision of services and the exercise of authority are prerequisites for citizen trust in the public service. The goal of these general ethical guidelines is to ensure that all state employees are aware of this. The ethical guidelines are to be of a general nature, rather than provide detailed rules. They are intended to provide general guidelines that call for reflection on the part of the individual employee. For example, the Ethical Guidelines for the Public Service provide guidance on how employees should act when former employees contact them.

The provisions included in the guidelines are not always exact, but rather specify legal standards. Norway has a number of legal rules (statutory and non-statutory) that have an impact on values and ethics in the public service. The ethical standards that apply at any given time have an impact on the framing of legislation and other regulations. From this perspective, the guidelines complement existing legal rules.

The guidelines have evolved from ethical values and norms of universal validity such as justice, loyalty, honesty, reliability, truthfulness and the golden "do unto others" rule.

Consequences of breaching the guidelines

Breaching the general Ethical Guidelines does not carry special sanctions, but, for example, breaches of the provisions that apply to conflicts of interest could result in a decision being declared invalid. An act or failure to act in the service could be considered a dereliction of duty, and could lead to service sanctions. An act or failure to act in the service could also be so serious that it could lead to prosecution and punitive sanctions. Clear-cut breaches of statutory provisions will normally also constitute breaches of ethical and administrative guidelines of universal validity.

Even if a civil servant does not breach a law or formal regulation, the breach of the Ethical Guidelines could be deterimental to his/her career. Where Ethical Guidelines have been made known throughout an organisation, not least to individuals, breaches of the guidelines will be a factor that can be emphasised, for example, in an overall assessment of the relevant public official's suitability for a position or in connection with an internal application for a new position, where it is fair to require compliance with the organisation's Ethical Guidelines.

Employers, managers and employees

As an employer (represented by the Ministry of Government Administration and Reform), the State has the ultimate responsibility for providing ethical guidelines and ensuring compliance. Top management in ministries and subordinate organisations bears special responsibility for follow up. This is primarily because managers, through their words, actions and management style, exert a strong influence on the culture and standards of conduct that apply in an organisation. Secondly, it is because top managers can be put in situations where choices and decisions call for ethical reflection and wisdom. Thirdly, it is because top managers are responsible for ensuring that the entire organisation is aware of the ethical standards that apply, and for ensuring that the organisation addresses any breaches of laws or regulations immediately in order to avoid the emergence of unfortunate customs or culture.

Individual employees are required to familiarise themselves with the provisions and instructions that apply to their positions at any given time, and they are personally responsible for the best possible compliance with the guidelines.

The legal context of guidelines: Their relationship with legislation

The guidelines were developed to complement the existing rules of law. Ensuring coherence of guidelines with relevant pieces of legislation was a particular consideration in the drafting process. Consequently, some of the most important rules of this area are specifically mentioned in the guidelines, namely:

- **The Public Administration Act** contains a number of administrative procedures that cover ethical aspects. Norway has provisions regarding the thoroughness of administrative decisions, among other things, that a case is to be explained as much as possible prior to administrative decisions. There are provisions about notification of the person(s) to which a case refers. The party shall also have an opportunity to make a statement before any decision is taken and has the right to appeal an administrative decision. The Public Administration Act also has competency rules intended to maintain trust in the public service. In the event that circumstances arise that can serve to weaken the impartiality of decision makers, the person in question must step aside. Moreover, the Public Administration Act contains rules about parties' right of access documents and the duty to provide guidance and confidentiality.
- **The Freedom of Information Act** has provisions regarding transparency and public access to government information and documents. These rules assign responsibilities and rights to administrative bodies and parties and thereby translate ethical principles into practical administrative procedures.

- **Non-statutory administrative principles,** for example knowledge about the misuse of authority, set standards regarding how judgement should be exercised. Public officials shall take into account all relevant considerations, treat identical cases equally, not take extraneous or arbitrary considerations into account and not adopt unreasonable decisions. Moreover, Norway has general non-statutory principles of "good practice".
- **The General Civil Penal Code** contains a provision on corruption and trading. Serious forms of corruption have a sentencing framework of up to ten years. The code contains rules about "felonies in the public sector".
- In this context, reference is also made to the **Human Rights Act** that gives a number of international conventions the same status as Norwegian Law, for the protection of human rights and fundamental freedom.
- There is also a paragraph in the **Civil Service Act** that forbids public officials to accept gifts, commissions, services or the like that is appropriated to, or intended by the donor to influence actions in their public service capacity.
- **The Working Environment Act** contains provisions about preserving the lives and health of the individual employees and ensuring the protection of the working environment. Among other things, employees have a duty to inform their employer, safety delegate and, insofar as necessary, other employees about faults or defects that could potentially endanger life and health, etc. In December 2005 the Ministry of Labour and Social Inclusion presented a proposal concerning new rules for whistle-blowing in the Working Environment Act. The proposal has now been made law, and gives employees a right to report corruption, breach of safety rules and other critical conditions in the organisation. The proposal also bans employers from punishing an employee for whistle-blowing.

Annexes to Chapter 5 are available on line at the links below:

5.A1. Post-Employment Guidelines for Politicians:
http://dx.doi.org/10.1787/735516772805

5.A2. Post-Employment Guidelines for the Public Service:
http://dx.doi.org/10.1787/735536866404

5.A3. Ethical Guidelines for the Public Service:
http://dx.doi.org/10.1787/735573105756

OECD PUBLISHING, 2, rue André-Pascal, 75775 PARIS CEDEX 16
PRINTED IN FRANCE
(42 2009 07 1 P) ISBN 978-92-64-05669-5 – No. 57033 2010